MASTERING THE HIRE

12 STRATEGIES TO IMPROVE YOUR ODDS OF FINDING THE BEST HIRE

CHAKA BOOKER

HarperCollins LEADERSHIP

AN IMPRINT OF HARPERCOLLINS

Published by HarperCollins Leadership, an imprint of HarperCollins Focus LLC.

Book design by Maria Fernandez, Neuwirth & Associates.

ISBN 978-1-4002-1641-3 (eBook)
ISBN 978-1-4002-1640-6 (TP)

Library of Congress Cataloging-in-Publication Data TK

Printed in the United States of America
19 20 21 22 23 LSC 5 4 3 2 1

MASTERING THE HIRE

for Oralia

CONTENTS

FOREWORD

BY ELI BROAD

*I*n my office, I keep a copy of *Against the Gods: The Remarkable Story of Risk* by Peter L. Bernstein. The book provides a historic account of the thinkers who studied risk and learned how to manage the odds. It documents how that ability has become a driver of success in the modern world. From the mathematical birthplace of risk in the Hindu-Arabic numbering system, to advances in probability theory during the 1700s, to recent research in behavioral economics, Bernstein makes a strong argument that effective decisionmakers are effective oddsmakers.

My earliest experiences with the odds were at the racetrack. I grew up in Detroit, raised by working class immigrants. My mother was a dressmaker. My father was a house painter who eventually ran two five-and-dime stores. He occasionally bet on horses and I sometimes tagged along. Later, as a student at Michigan State University, I was making ends meet by selling garbage disposals door-to-door and working as a drill-press operator at Packard Motor. I decided to try my luck with the horses. I was good with numbers but initially was barely breaking even. Then I started following the trainers, pestering them with questions. Soon my winnings began to outpace my losses.

Understanding the relationship between research and risk was an important early lesson. By the time I was twenty-three I had founded my first company, today known as KB Home. I bought my second company for $52 million and transformed it from a sleepy insurance firm into the retirement savings giant SunAmerica, which we sold for $18 billion. As the founder of two Fortune 500 companies, understanding the odds has been integral to my success time and again. The other key factor has been understanding talent.

When I first started hiring for KB Home, I conducted the interviews myself. I would fly in and out of cities searching for talented professionals willing to join a company they had never heard of in an industry that wasn't exactly glamorous. My approach to interviewing was straightforward. To this day, I focus on understanding how clearly a candidate thinks and how much knowledge they have about the work we're doing. Determining if they have confidence, ambition, and drive continue to be a priority. I learned a lot about hiring from those early experiences. I learned resumes don't tell the full story. I learned hiring people who are different than me helps keep my viewpoints relevant. I learned when to trust my gut and take a risk on someone untried. I wasn't a perfect interviewer, but I learned to beat the odds.

A lot has changed in the world since I first started building companies. But talent still matters. An organization is only as strong as its people. Identifying those people takes more than good fortune. To consistently make the right hiring decisions, you must understand how to influence the probability of success. The book in your hands captures that relationship and aims it at interviewing. It is an incredible resource for anyone facing the most important business decision you can make, "Do I hire this person?"

The author, Chaka Booker, knows a thing or two about beating the odds. He grew up in Los Angeles, also from humble beginnings. His father was a Marine Corps veteran. His mother was a teacher. Austerity and discipline ruled their home. He went to public school, wore second-hand clothes and rode the bus everywhere. When he was in the tenth grade, his parents separated, and through a set of difficult circumstances, he ended up living on his own.

With a level of determination rare at any age, Chaka supported himself through high school by taking every job you could imagine—grocery bagger, busboy, cashier, yard hand. He even sold insurance by phone. Los

Angeles can be tough place for a teenager on his own and the odds were certainly stacked against him. But he graduated from high school, set his sights higher, and kept beating the odds. He worked his way through college at UCLA, where he double majored in psychology and economics. He started a small business and followed that with an MBA from Stanford.

I met Chaka when we hired him fresh out of business school. He was smart, entrepreneurial, and had life experiences that made him think differently than others. Anyone who knows me knows I like unconventional thinkers. He fit the bill for what we needed in an organization we had recently created, The Broad Center.

My business career has allowed me to dedicate myself full time to philanthropy. The Eli and Edythe Broad Foundation has given more than $600 million to support public education. We created the Broad Institute with MIT and Harvard to focus on genomics research to cure major diseases. The Broad Museum houses two world-class art collections that we built and has free general admission.

The Broad Center was spun out from the foundation in response to challenges we saw in the social sector. Several years of grant-making had taught us that social sector organizations faced management challenges not so different from those in the private sector. Many of the organizations were saddled with operational inefficiencies, antiquated systems, or both. On one end of the spectrum were immense enterprises like the NYC Department of Education, with a $25 billion budget and 135,000 employees. On the other end were smaller organizations operating on a shoestring. In high demand at all points of the spectrum were talented people with skills in strategy, operations, finance, human resources, and management.

The Broad Center was created to meet that demand. The center operates highly selective leadership programs dedicated to recruiting and developing professionals across the country and helping them take on management positions in public education. The complexity of leadership needed to manage public entities that address the needs of children in every socioeconomic status, geographic terrain, and family structure is enormous. Historical and structural inequities are deeply entrenched, and students are the ones who pay the price. Passion helps, but fighting the status quo is not for the faint of the heart. It requires a type of talent that is hard to find, and harder yet to assess. It can't be left to chance.

Unearthing unique talent requires an intentional and disciplined process. Every year, The Broad Center runs applicants through a gauntlet of interviews and assessments. Written essays. Video responses. Phone interviews. A small group advances to an entire day filled with multiple in-person interviews, case studies, and group exercises. An even smaller group then advances to interview with the organizations who partner with the center. By the end, less than 3 percent of applicants are accepted into the center's programs.

For more than fifteen years, that selection process has been designed, analyzed, refined, redesigned, and deployed by Chaka and his team. Understanding talent and the many shapes it can take is his expertise. He has crisscrossed the country, spending thousands of hours on university campuses, at human capital conferences, and in interview rooms. He has assessed talent from higher education, Fortune 500s, K–12 school systems, startups, leadership programs, the military, and everything between. He's assembled and trained teams of interviewers from across sectors and disciplines. Each of them brings their own expertise, which in turn shapes and strengthens Chaka's approach.

Chaka is now a managing director for The Broad Center, which has cultivated nearly a thousand leaders. Ninety percent of our program graduates continue to work in the social sector and 92 percent of their supervisors report they would hire them again without hesitation. In the world of talent, that level of accuracy is rare. It isn't accidental. It can be replicated.

Whether you are a hiring manager, HR personnel, CEO, search consultant, team manager, team member, novice, or expert interviewer, you need to make the right hiring decisions, and more often. Captured in this book are a set of strategies and practices which will increase your accuracy. It is as practical as it is thoughtful. You will find some of the ideas unconventional. A willingness to take risk will be necessary.

That is precisely why I encourage you to keep reading. At its heart, this book is about decisionmaking and how to tilt the odds. As history has shown, that ability is a hallmark of those who are successful.

THE COIN TOSS

*W*hat is the purpose of a job interview? According to Frank L. Schmidt, a psychologist renowned for his research in personnel selection, the value of an interview lies in its "predictive validity"—the ability to predict future job performance. That is an assertion few would argue with. The logical next question then is, do job interviews predict job performance?

To answer this question, Schmidt partnered with psychologist John E. Hunter, an expert in research methodology. To measure the predictive relationship between interview performance and job performance, they conducted a meta-analysis on eighty-five years of research on personnel selection. Included in the analysis were nineteen different methods for assessing talent. The results were sobering. At best, the methods had a predictive validity of 54 percent. For unstructured interviews* it was 38 percent and for structured interviews it stood at 51 percent.[1]

Fast forward more than two decades and little has changed. Scour the internet for statistics on hiring and you'll find new studies with similar results.[2] In some cases, the results are worse. A recent Gallup

---

* A structured interview contains predetermined questions, usually asked in the same order. Unstructured interviews tend to be casual, unrehearsed, and questions are not set in advance.

study found that when it comes to management talent, companies fail to choose the right candidate 82 percent of the time.[3] While interviews aren't the sole input leading to these outcomes, they are a primary one. And if you include marginal performers who do just well enough to not get fired and candidates who didn't interview well enough to get the job but would have been great, then the conclusion you can draw isn't an inspiring one.

The reason for those odds is simple. The two people who face each other at the interview table, don't do it often enough to do it well.

THE INTERVIEW TABLE

Let's think about that interview table. On one side sits the interviewer. If they work for Human Resources, they likely oversee a range of responsibilities, of which hiring is one of many. Within hiring, interviewing is also just one work stream among others. HR professionals rarely get the resources and focus needed for interviewing to become an area of expertise.

If not from HR, interviewers are usually the managers or colleagues the candidate may eventually work with. While it is a good idea to ask them to serve as interviewers, it is a bad idea to assume that because they know the skills required for the job they will be good at assessing others for those skills. At best, they have some of the tools—a set of criteria, a corresponding set of questions—and occasional exposure to assessment techniques.

As a result, decisions aren't based on the candidate's skills, but on personal preferences, gut feelings, communication style, and other faulty heuristics. Still, on any given day, someone is deputized, handed a candidate's resume, and asked to make a key organizational decision using a skill which isn't their strength—interviewing.

On the other side of the table sits the candidate, a person who interviews even less often. According to the Bureau of Labor Statistics, on average, people switch employers every 4.3 years (for those aged twenty-five to thirty-four it's 2.8 years).[4] In other words, the candidate who begins to make the interview rounds hasn't done so in three or four years. The chances are high that they're going to be a little rusty. To prepare for this, candidates get ready the way anyone would when faced with answering questions on short notice: They cram.

They think of examples that will match questions they aren't certain will be asked. They memorize statistics and facts about the hiring organization, hoping they will be relevant. They prepare answers for why they want this job, how much a shoebox full of quarters weighs, and why they chose to major in anthropology. They hold all this in their heads as they enter the interview room. That's assuming they prepared.

We now have two people at a table. The interviewer, with a vague understanding of what she is doing. The candidate, trying to explain what he is capable of doing. The interviewer makes assumptions about the candidate. The candidate crafts answers hoping they lead to the right assumptions. The interviewer reads a question and thinks, "Why am I asking this?" The candidate hears the question and thinks, "Why are they asking me that?"

That's what a typical interview is. Two people at a table doing something neither of them is great at doing. What are the odds of a great decision coming from that table?

About the same as tossing a coin.

Anyone satisfied with the 50 percent success rate uncovered by Schmidt and Hunter's research should stop doing round after round of interviews and simply do one round of interviews to weed out clearly bad candidates. They should then toss a coin to make the decision. That would be the logical thing to do. Less work, same results. The problem is those same results carry the emotional toll of having to fire people, the financial cost of having to rehire, and the organizational turmoil associated with low performance.

The smarter thing to do is learn how to shift the odds and avoid those outcomes.

THE BELIEF

Despite Schmidt and Hunter's findings and countless studies conducted since then, people still believe that a candidate's performance during an interview will predict their performance on the job. Destroying that belief is the first step toward increasing the accuracy of your interviews.

That won't be easy. The belief is remarkably resilient. It is common knowledge that some candidates interview well and then don't perform well. Everyone also knows that some candidates have average interviews and still end up strong performers. That reality doesn't matter; the belief endures.

You can hear it in the casual comments we make as we prepare to meet a candidate, "I hope this candidate interviews well." That hope suggests if the candidate interviews well, they will do the job well. When we make a bad hire, the belief tiptoes into our narrative again, "I don't get what happened, he interviewed really well." If we don't hire someone but they do well somewhere else, the belief reappears, this time dressed up as surprise, "Wow. That's strange because with us, she didn't interview well at all."

The entire hiring process is built on this belief. It sits at the core of every decision, quietly eating away at the odds. The belief lives because we need it to live. It protects us from a truth we don't want to acknowledge. Pry open the belief and inside you will find a deception. Like all great deceptions, it is simple.

The truth is, there actually is a connection between interview performance and job performance. But it isn't the candidate's interview performance that affects their job performance. *It's the interviewer's performance that affects the candidate's job performance.*

When Schmidt and Hunter discovered the weak relationship between interview performance and job performance it wasn't because of the candidate's skill at interviewing—it was because of the interviewer's skill at interviewing.

You must hold firmly to this truth, so the old belief can die. This doesn't absolve candidates of their responsibility. It simply heightens yours and means you have more control over the odds than you realize.

THE BLACK BOX

Organizations don't need candidates that interview well. They need candidates that can do the job well. That means they need *interviewers* that interview well. It is the interviewer who must have a great interview, not the candidate.

> Organizations don't need candidates that interview well. They need candidates that can do the job well.

For most interviewers, the relationship between interview practices and accurate hiring decisions is a black box where the effect of one on the other is a mystery. We can all point to candidates we interviewed who turned out great. We can also point to those who didn't. But can we point to what we did during the interview that led to either result? That's the black box. Without knowing what is inside that box, we can't consistently replicate our successes. We can't beat the odds.

From a statistical standpoint, to prove a hypothesis about cause and effect you need large sample sizes and consistent reproduction of the same outcomes. From the standpoint of interviewing, this translates into needing high volume exposure to how candidates interview, tracking what you did during the interview, and evidence of how they later perform as employees. The sporadic nature of interviewing is not conducive to this type of insight. So, the black box remains.

My interviewing experience has been different than most. For more than a decade, I've worked squarely in the center of the black box.

I work for The Broad Center, a national organization that runs leadership development programs focused on identifying and developing talent. Because we collect data on our participants, including interview scores, 360 feedback, supervisor ratings, and organizational surveys, we have the benefit of knowing how well candidates interviewed and how well they performed on their jobs. Since we run a highly structured interview process, we also know what we consistently did or didn't do during the process.

Within that environment, I've reviewed more than five thousand resumes, read just as many essays, conducted nearly three thousand interviews, and have reflected on every one of them. I've analyzed every mistake, questioned every belief, refined, experimented, studied, documented, and reflected again. Across the years, I've co-interviewed with and learned from some of the best interviewers from organizations known for talent—IBM, Procter & Gamble, McKinsey, Google.

To better understand candidates and myself, I've grounded my practices in research from the fields of psychology, cognitive science, behavioral economics, and a range of other sciences.

Over time I've identified which assessment methods are most effective at predicting who a candidate is and what they can do. Beating the odds has been about recognizing those patterns. As behavioral economists would say, there is a rhythm and regularity to human behavior. What you'll find in this book are the patterns, rhythms, and regularities of successful interviewing distilled into strategies and practices that anyone can learn. It blends science, an understanding of human behavior, and the firsthand experience of expert interviewers.

The book has five parts. My recommendation is to pause after reading each part. You don't need to agree with every strategy nor implement every practice. Instead, determine which ones resonate most with you and take note of them. Then begin to layer them into your current interview process. Get comfortable with them. Then layer in a few more. You may not need all of them. Use this book to rethink how you make decisions. Then use the relevant practices to shift toward better hiring outcomes.

What you won't find in this book is any sentence stating, *"Do X and your odds will increase by Y percent."* Although interviews can be predictive, humans can't be placed into an algorithm. No one ever knows with 100 percent certainty whether the person in front of them is right for the job. Certainty isn't the goal. A belief in certainty can be as dangerous as a reliance on luck. Every hiring decision you make will carry some level of risk. There is always a gamble. But as any oddsmaker will tell you, when you gamble, there are two types of games you can play. Games of chance and games of skill.

A quote from Schmidt and Hunter's research paper highlights this truth, "Employers must make hiring decisions; they have no choice about that. But they can choose which methods to use in making those decisions." Interviewing should never be a game of chance. Hiring does not have to be a coin toss. Regardless of your starting point, you can increase the odds of finding great talent. That is the goal.

• PART 1 •

REDUCING INTERFERENCE

An interview is an interactive process. That seems obvious and innocuous. Except when you consider that an interaction is defined as a "reciprocal action or influence" and within that reciprocity there is a lot of noise. Most people are unaware of the psychological, emotional, and physical factors that take control of them as soon as they interact with another person.

The moment you step into the interview room, human nature kicks in and you and the candidate instinctually begin reading each other. Signals, social cues, and assumptions fill the space between the two of you, influencing your behaviors and your decisionmaking processes. Some of the signals are interpreted inaccurately or have nothing to do with assessing the candidate—they are interference. Your job is to understand and minimize the noise that interferes with an accurate read of the candidate's talent.

INTUITION, KNOW THY PLACE

A common phenomenon in candidate selection is a stubborn reliance by interviewers on their intuition.[1] We would all like to believe our instincts are razor sharp and our gut reactions are in tune with reality. Interestingly, science may actually support this belief.

Research published in the *Journal of Personality and Social Psychology* found that first impressions tend to be incredibly accurate.[2] In the study, undergraduates were shown muted thirty-second videos of instructors they hadn't met, teaching a class. The undergraduate's assessment of these instructors was found to be highly correlated (.76) with the assessments made by a separate group of students who had taken a sixteen-week class with the instructors *in person*.

The phenomenon was dubbed "thin-slicing." The idea that small windows of exposure allow for accurate assessments has been replicated in multiple studies with different demographics and controls. The discoveries in this area were the foundation for Malcolm Gladwell's best-selling book, *Blink: The Power of Thinking Without Thinking*.

From an interviewing standpoint, this should be revolutionary. Everyone who has ever interviewed anyone has had an immediate first impression, usually within the first few minutes. Perhaps the gap between perception and reality is smaller than we thought. Perhaps we are spending far too much time with candidates.

If only it were that easy.

There is good reason to be extremely cautious about first impressions. All the studies indicate that first impressions are subject to stereotyping and prejudice. These preconceptions, commonly associated with race, gender, and other forms of identity, lead to a lack of diverse perspectives and experiences in organizations. The impact of first impressions are problematic beyond even the traditional definitions of identity. Stereotyping and prejudice describe any belief you cast upon an entire group. I've co-interviewed with people who have beliefs about how a resume should look. Anything other than Times New Roman or Arial font is too creative for their tastes. Before the candidate has even entered the room, a first impression—informed by the interviewer's belief—exists.

First impressions impact decisionmaking. They are often instinctual and based on what matters to that specific interviewer. But what if the interviewer's interpretation is not what matters most to the organization or the role being hired for? If they are not aligned, the first impression can lead to the wrong hiring decision.

The goal is not to develop absolute objectivity during interviewing. That can be just as troublesome because psychological, emotional, and physical reactions exist for a reason. Sometimes first impressions are accurate. It's not that intuition doesn't have a place, but that you must know its place. To increase the odds of making a strong decision, you need to manage subjectivity, so you can determine the relevance of a first impression.

It's not that intuition doesn't
have a place, but that you
must know its place.

PARK YOUR FIRST IMPRESSIONS

The problem to resolve is not whether first impressions exist. Nor is the question whether they have an effect on our decisions during interviews. Research indicates the answer to both questions is yes. A trio of researchers, each from a different university, worked together to address this question by conducting a study on decisionmaking during job interviews.[3] The study was designed to learn how quickly interviewers make decisions about job applicants. 25.5 percent made their decision within the first five minutes. Sixty percent made their decision within the first fifteen minutes.

It is impossible to not have a first impression, even if that impression is neutral. Eliminating first impressions would go against human nature, so don't try. Instead, go in the other direction. Acknowledge that first impressions exist and then use a practice that allows you to determine if the early impressions are accurate and relevant. That practice is called "parking your first impression." You park your first impression by documenting it the moment it happens. That practice moves it from the brain, where it quietly impacts decisions, and places it in the open where it can be examined.

Personal Protocol

Parking your first impression allows you to capture it and make it a data point to be discussed later. To get a feel for it, begin by using the practice independently as you interview. It is simple and takes five seconds of preparation. Before you are about to interview someone, draw the following on the bottom of their resume or the document on which you will take notes.

Yes   **I don't know**   **No**

Once the interview begins, within the first few moments, make a mark on the line indicating what your first impression is:

- Yes, they are a strong candidate
- I don't know if they are a strong candidate
- No, they are not a strong candidate

This protocol acknowledges your first impression and allows you to actively "check it off" as an assessment. This imposed discipline helps you separate your first impression from the remainder of the interview when you may not have the self-discipline to take this step yourself.

Now that you have logged your first impression, *your job is to ignore it*. This part of the process is critical otherwise you will seek evidence during the interview to justify your first impression. In psychology, this is called *confirmation bias*. To avoid it, remind yourself that your first impression is a single data point to be considered *after* the interview along with other evidence.* Physically logging your first impression is a reminder that it exists and that it will taint the evidence you are collecting unless you put it aside.

This practice will have an interesting effect on you. First, you will begin to realize how often you do have an opinion before you've gathered enough answers to have one. Second, the documentation allows you to realize that sometimes your first impression aligns with how well the candidate interviewed and sometimes it doesn't. Those moments when it doesn't are the most important part of this practice. Those are the candidates with underestimated talent who had the odds against them from the start. By putting aside your first impression, you even the odds and open the door to finding unrecognized talent.

---

*   First impressions are subject to confirmation bias and the anchoring effect. We'll return to both cognitive errors in a few pages with a specific practice for managing them.

Over time, you will find yourself increasingly marking "I don't know" at the start of the interview. Because if you did know, why would you waste time interviewing them? Through consistent use of this protocol, you will begin to more quickly notice your first impressions and will develop the habit of controlling them in the moment.

This is the shift you want. It allows you to cut through interference and focus on who the candidate is, not who you think they are.

Team Protocol

Once you've implemented this practice on your own, turn it into a protocol that all your interviewers can use. Include the following template as the first page in the question packet that your interviewers use for the interview.

Before beginning the interview, mark your answer to the following question. *On which side of the mid-line does your first impression of the candidate fall?*

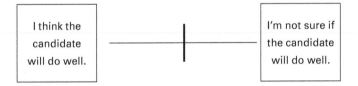

Now that you have logged your first impression, your job is to ignore it.
Your first impression is a single data point, don't allow it to impact the rest of the interview.
During the remainder of the interview, resist temptation to justify your first impression.
Only assess the candidate on the questions you ask them.
The final result may or may not align with your first impression.

There are two things to note about this template. First, the diagram only asks on which side of the mid-line the first impression falls.

Second, the last line of instruction explains that the first impression may or may not align with the final result. Both instructions must be included to prevent the self-fulfilling prophecy that confirmation bias leads to. You want to avoid forcing a commitment to one end of the spectrum or the other. Anyone interviewing must remain open to the possibility that their first impression may be different than what happens during the interview.

It is critical to make this second point clear to anyone interviewing. Talk through these instructions line by line with your interviewers and ensure that everyone understands the underlying concept and potential risk if not done well.

During the post-interview discussion, the facilitator should acknowledge the first impressions interviewers may have had. For example:

> **Lead Interviewer:** I want to take a moment to acknowledge that you've parked your first impression. As we discuss the content of the interview, feel free to reference your first impression in one of two ways. First, if you think your first impression was relevant to the job being hired for. Or, if you feel your first impression may have influenced you one way or another. By raising it, we can discuss it as a group . . .

This creates a space to discuss the first impressions and treat them as data points. Once they are in the open, the group can determine their relevance. Now that you know how to capture first impressions, let's learn what to do with them.

PRACTICE:
KNOWING WHEN TO TRUST FIRST IMPRESSIONS

It is important to remember your goal is not to capture first impressions because you know they are inaccurate. Your goal is to capture them because you *don't know* if they are inaccurate. In some instances, first impressions can be accurate and relevant, and you don't want to lose valuable information.

> It is important to remember your goal is not to capture first impressions because you know they are inaccurate. Your goal is to capture them because you don't know if they are inaccurate.

Cognitive psychologist Dr. Gary Klein discovered that first impressions can be most trusted when the impression comes from someone who has expertise assessing the situation at hand.[4] In *Blink*, Gladwell gives the example of a firefighter who instinctually knew to order his men out of a house moments before the floor collapsed. In this case, the firefighter's instinct was rooted in years of knowledge and experiences that were directly applicable to the decision he had to make.

Even in the original "thin-slicing" studies the importance of expertise plays a role. It is no surprise that undergraduates, who by that point in their life have been in school for at least thirteen years, have a strong intuitive sense of what makes a good instructor. They have spent countless hours with instructors of varying quality across multiple environments. They have been absorbing what good and bad instruction looks like. Their first impression is very valid for the assessment they were asked to make.

In my early years at The Broad Center, I would often spend day after day interviewing candidates. By my fourth year, I could tell within twenty minutes whether a candidate was cut out for the work. At that point in my career I had interviewed hundreds of candidates and knew which ones had gone on to success, and which ones had struggled, and why. That longitudinal perspective allowed me to connect the dots and know what success in the work looked like at the interview stage.

For that reason, I started to do twenty-minute interviews with candidates at the final stage. If we were uncertain about a candidate, my assessment could help push the decision one way or the other. Perfection wasn't the goal: I still made mistakes, but the odds of making a mistake were much lower.

If you have an interviewer with a track record of accurately assessing talent on your team, then trust that person's ability. Their impression, paired with the more formal assessments, will lead to stronger decisions. To be clear, this is different than trusting the first impression of an interviewer who only knows the job well. Knowing how to do your job well is an expertise, but a very different one than required for accurate assessments. It bears repeating: *To trust first impressions, the interviewer must have a track record of accurately assessing for the job.* Their quick assessment is based on years of firsthand data collection and you should leverage it.

The other occasion to trust first impressions is if the majority of your interviewers have similar first impressions. This realization comes to light during the post-interview discussion because once people have parked their first impression, they often refer to it. Look out for the moments when someone mentions their first impression, and someone else in the room says, "I had the same reaction." This will then be followed by a few others who picked up on the same thing. Those moments must be discussed because you may have a relevant first impression.

When multiple people echo the same impression, pause and ask the following questions:

- How would you describe what you picked up on?
- Does it matter for this role? Is it relevant?
- Are we all picking up on this just because we are used to a certain type of person and want to remain comfortable?

The last question is important because the "first impression" felt by multiple people could still be an irrelevant bias—race, gender, or otherwise—that keeps an organization insular. This can be a difficult discussion to have. It is the responsibility of the facilitator and any senior leader in the room to model the courage to have these conversations.

If you are the leader, question your own motives, and make sure the group's first impressions aren't blocking access to talented people because they are different than what the organization is used to. These kinds of conversations can often be breakthrough conversations that lead to stronger decisions and change the organization for the better.*

PRACTICE:
KEEP RESETTING

Every question you ask causes your assessment of the candidate to evolve, and if you are not careful, solidify too soon. That is why more than 25 percent of interviewers in the previously mentioned study made their decision in the first five minutes and 60 percent made a decision within fifteen minutes. Parking your first impression improves those percentages, but each answer the candidate provides still builds momentum in one direction or another. A few initial good answers will create a halo effect and any answer that follows will sound better. Initial bad answers have the opposite effect.

If the decision made in the first fifteen minutes is accurate, then this isn't a concern. If that decision isn't accurate then the noise between who the candidate is and who you think they are just keeps increasing. The problem is—in the moment—you don't know if it is accurate.

You have to bring that momentum to a standstill.

Making a decision within fifteen minutes of an interview is less than halfway through. If the remainder of the interview wasn't used to help make the decision, then what was it used for? Cognitive science tells us it was likely used to confirm what the interviewer came to believe in the first fifteen minutes.

---

* Part 4 addresses in more depth how to manage complex biases, such as those based on race or gender.

This phenomenon is a result of two mental heuristics—anchoring effect and confirmation bias.[5] Anchoring occurs when a person relies too heavily on initial information they receive to make decisions. Confirmation bias is the tendency to interpret new evidence as confirmation of existing beliefs or theories. Subsequent information that doesn't fit the initial input is often discounted. Anchoring happens early in the interview, confirmation happens in the remainder.

To stop the momentum, you must assess each question in isolation while also keeping your overall assessment of the candidate undecided throughout the interview. This requires a mental reset after each answer the candidate provides. If a candidate doesn't do well on a question, tell yourself, "Not a great answer, but I'm going to reset and stay neutral as we head into the next one." If they do great on an answer, remind yourself, "Great answer, and now let's reset to bring it back to neutral before the next question."

This practice of resetting takes mental muscle, but it is a strength that can be deliberately built. Once developed, it allows you to collect a much larger amount of insight. You've effectively extended the window in which you are gaining insight on the candidate, all of which shifts the odds toward a better decision.

CANDIDATES DON'T ANSWER QUESTIONS. THEY ANSWER PEOPLE

*C*ontrolling the influence of first impressions on your decisions is only part of the battle against interference. Influence flows both ways. You must also control the influence you have on the candidate during the interview.

Social cues are verbal and nonverbal hints between people which guide our behavior by clarifying meaning and intention. This information is often processed without our consciousness. They are a characteristic of human nature developed to help us recognize whether we are being accepted or rejected by those we are interacting with. Research done at the University of Chicago has shown that people who are focused on connecting with their counterpart are particularly accurate at decoding the social cues the other person is exhibiting.[1]

In other words, candidates are constantly reading interviewers for cues. Not only can they tell if you like or dislike an answer, they are good at adjusting accordingly. Because of this dynamic, the interviewer can unknowingly do more than just gather answers from the candidate. If not careful, the interviewer can push the candidate to provide certain answers.

The following practices are aimed at managing your behavior so that candidates' answers are theirs alone—not answers you co-created with them.

INTERVIEW LIKE A POKER PLAYER

If you've ever watched poker tournaments, you've seen professionals whose entire careers are built around beating the odds. Winning at the poker table isn't just skill at playing cards, it also requires a deep understanding of human nature. Among other things, professional poker players understand social cues and hone the ability to read their opponents' faces to help determine their next moves. They also control their own face because they know their opponents are also reading them for signals to interpret. Hence the ability to keep a "poker face."

Maintaining a consistent expression isn't just for Vegas high-rollers, it is an essential skill for an interviewer. The study done at the University of Chicago found that as the importance of connecting with a counterpart rose, so did the ability to read their facial emotions. Candidates know that their future lies in your hands and your facial expressions are the primary source of information on how they are doing. Their adjustments to those signals interfere with your ability to assess who they truly are or what they are truly thinking.

If we favor someone from the outset, we'll send cues to help them. If we don't favor them, we won't. The candidates receiving positive cues will gain momentum from the positive energy you are giving them. This gives them an advantage that other candidates might not get. If you don't connect with the candidate immediately, your face and body language are likely to show it. You may give them fewer positive cues or even give them cues that they are doing poorly. Instead of learning about the candidate's skills and aptitude, you'll be learning how they react to a person frowning at them, or how they react to a person yawning and checking their watch. If you exhibited the same indifference or dissatisfaction toward a candidate you liked, their performance might also change. This is how you end up missing talent.

To control for the impact your behavior has on the candidate's performance, you must present the same facial expressions *across* candidates. This does not mean, however, you should present everyone with the emotionless expression that is commonly associated with a poker face.

To determine what expression you should be exhibiting, let's return to the game of poker but through the lens of cognitive science.

A team of researchers lead by cognitive psychologist Dr. Erick Schlicht conducted an experiment to determine the facial expression which had the best odds for winning at poker.[2] In the experiment, participants played hundreds of one-shot rounds of a simplified version of Texas hold 'em poker against hundreds of different opponents. The participants played only one round against each opponent and therefore couldn't use past behavior to make decisions. The only information they had was the cards in their hands and cues from their opponent's face. The opponents displayed a range of expressions, including a neutral expression.

Across a range of other controls, surprisingly the poker face that won the most was not neutral, but one that portrayed trustworthiness. As we'll discuss further in Part 2, building trust is a key element to effective interviewing. A facial expression that maintains consistency across candidates and builds trust with each candidate is the goal. If you are wondering what trustworthiness looks like, the answer is simple: It is an expression that is slightly positive and friendly. If that still doesn't conjure up the right image, then simply present the smallest of smiles, a slight upturn at the corners of your mouth. For optimal results, accompany this expression with a set of standard positive responses for all candidates:

- Give head nods and small encouraging smiles during the interview.
- Give verbal signs of affirmation that seem positive but are neutral. For example, at the end of the candidate's answer or even during the answer, the interviewer should say "Got it." or "I understand."

You want to gather accurate information from the person and being encouraging increases the odds of that happening. Your expression and affirmative responses acknowledge that you are listening and are in a positive mood, but the comments themselves are neutral. They don't indicate that the answer is right or wrong, just that you hear it. That acknowledgment makes the interview more of a natural conversation, which works in your favor.

The paradox is that your consistency of expression and response will *not* feel natural to you. It may make you feel self-conscious and inauthentic. Keep in the mind, the candidate doesn't know that you are saying the exact same things and doing the same head nods and smile with everyone. The downside of you feeling inauthentic is outweighed by the benefit of putting every candidate through a signal-free process. This increases the odds of candidates' answers being what you need to know as opposed to what they thought you wanted to hear.

PRACTICE:
PRE-DETERMINE YOUR BEHAVIOR
AND STAY CONSISTENT

How you feel about the candidate affects more than your facial expression and body language. It also impacts explicit behaviors such as how you deliver questions, the amount of time you give a candidate to respond, and how you respond to candidates' answers. This in turn will affect how they react. Your *ability* to understand the candidate is impacted by your *willingness* to understand the candidate.

> Your ability to understand
> the candidate is impacted
> by your willingness to
> understand the candidate.

Early in my interviewing experience I noticed that sometimes I would rephrase a question if the candidate seemed they didn't initially understand it. Without prompting, I gave them a second version of the question for clarity. Sometimes if a candidate gave an average answer I didn't probe as much. I'd give them a break, thinking to myself, "Yeah, I know what she meant." Or, I would probe until I got a better answer. But I didn't do this for everyone. For some candidates I was tougher. I was less supportive. I didn't probe for a better answer. An average answer was marked as average. If I did have to probe to get a better answer, I held it against them and marked them a little lower.

After I started the practice of parking my first impressions, I began to see a pattern in my behavior. If I had a favorable first impression of a candidate, then I was more lenient. I was more willing to give them the benefit of the doubt or help them make sense of their answer. Even though I was capturing the first impression and mentally putting it aside to be discussed later, my *physical* behavior was still impacting the interview process. It became my goal to make my interview behavior consistent, so every candidate was being interviewed by the same "me."

Once I became aware of this, I began noticing the same inconsistent behavior in other interviewers. Over the years, I've co-interviewed with countless interviewers. I've witnessed variance in interviewer behavior manifest most prominently in the same two ways it did for me: the willingness to rephrase a question (or not), and the number of follow-up questions asked to clarify an answer. To control this variance, you simply need to plan ahead.

Before the interview, decide whether you will rephrase your questions and do it that same way for every candidate. Similarly, predetermine the maximum number of follow-up questions you will ask and consistently apply this rule to every candidate. If you don't commit to that on the front end, you will ask the candidate you are subconsciously (or consciously) rooting for a different number of questions than the candidate you aren't rooting for. This may feel rigid and represent a constraint.

You may feel there legitimately are times when you need to do go above the maximum to really understand a candidate and wouldn't want to artificially limit yourself. That is understandable. There are times when I break these rules and ask more questions of some candidates because it is needed to best understand them. But because I now have rules, when I do bend them, an internal voice says, "Are you doing this because you like the candidate and want them to do well, or because you don't understand the answer?" Sometimes the answer is, "I legitimately need time to dig in here." But sometimes the answer is, "Yeah, I know . . . this person is bombing. But I want them to do well. If I just ask this question a different way . . . yeah, I know . . . stay consistent . . . I've spent enough time on this question, move on . . . ."

Predetermining how you will behave with all candidates and sticking to your plan allows every candidate to meet the same version of you. At first, both practices in this chapter will feel robotic and overly scripted. As you become accustomed to the practices, you'll realize that you can minimize the signals you send and still have a natural conversation. Those who are new to this type of approach may argue that it lacks authenticity. That may be true in ordinary settings, but this isn't an ordinary setting. This is an interview.

During an interview, presenting a different version of yourself to different candidates is a form of self-deception. You believe you are meeting the candidate and learning about them through your questions. Instead you are meeting a candidate reacting to you and your level of willingness to engage. You believe you are being authentic, when you are being the opposite. During an interview, consistency is authenticity, and it will get you a step closer to accurate decisionmaking.

During an interview, consistency is authenticity, and it will get you a step closer to accurate decisionmaking.

THE RIGHT QUESTION ASKED WRONG, IS THE WRONG QUESTION

*W*e don't only send signals to candidates through social cues and explicit behaviors, we also send them through the structure of the questions we ask. Behavioral interview questions generally contain some signal indicating what the answer should be. Very few candidates enter an interview intending to tell outright lies. They come prepared to tell their stories with examples of what they've accomplished. It isn't until they are presented with leading questions that they feel the pressure to provide examples that match signals they receive.

In an effort to give the right answer, they may morph examples of less relevant work experiences to make them more relevant to the question asked. This dynamic pushes the candidate away from the truth. It makes it difficult to decipher if a great answer was grounded in the candidate's actual skill or the result of the candidate being led to what the answer should be.

For example, a typical behavioral interview question is written as follows:

- Tell me about a time when you had to influence someone to take an action that they may otherwise not have taken.

Upon hearing this question, the candidate immediately knows that the right answer involves some form of "influencing someone to take an action that they may otherwise not have taken." And, no surprise, most candidates will come up with an answer, whether they have done this or not. If you next ask them:

- Give me an example of a time that you had to learn something quickly.

The candidate will know that the right answer involves them demonstrating they have learned quickly, whether they have had to learn quickly or not. Very rarely, will a candidate say, *"Nope, I've never done that. Next question please . . . . Hmmm, I've never done that either . . . . Let's try the next one."*

Truth and lies live on opposite ends of the same road. The path between them is made of variations of the truth. Each variation becomes less factual than the next as you move from one end to the other. Honesty also lives on this road and is what points people back toward the truth. Unfortunately, most interview questions contain noise that makes it difficult for candidates to be honest. While you may not hear lies during an interview, question design can push candidates toward that end of the road, and you may not hear the truth either. Instead you'll hear variations and you won't know how far from the truth they are.

Most people believe they can detect when someone isn't telling the truth. But science tells us otherwise. Coincidentally, the odds of you knowing when someone isn't telling the truth are also a coin toss at 54 percent.[1] To make things worse, research also tells us that even when we detect an untruth, we convince ourselves otherwise.[2] Fortunately, questions can be designed to promote honesty, rather than interfere with it, and candidates can be pointed toward the truth.

PRACTICE:
GO TO KANSAS

The first step to designing great questions is to not waste time designing them from scratch. A lot of smart people have spent a lot of time designing questions for every type of competency. Don't reinvent the wheel. Borrow the wheel and fix it.

Google is known for its forward-thinking talent practices. To improve their internal hiring and support high quality hiring decisions, they created a bank of questions that their employees have access to when interviewing. This tool isn't available to the public. But don't fret. Just click your heels three times.

The Kansas Department of Administration has also developed a powerful tool for generating interview questions. Not only do they provide over four hundred questions, they have a user-friendly platform that lets you pick the competencies you want to interview for. It then generates a set of questions, an interview guide, a rubric, and a set of eighteen follow-up questions. You don't have to fly to Kansas to access the platform. It's open to the public via their website.[3]

Even when pulled from the best resources, most questions still tend to be filled with signals. Once you've selected your questions, your next step is to improve their ability to gather the information you need.

PRACTICE:
REMOVE THE SIGNALS

Think of the candidate as a person who is selling you a house. As a home buyer, you can walk through a house to inspect what is in great shape and what will need repairs. In this analogy, the house is the candidate's experiences, except all the rooms are locked: The candidates won't give you the keys and won't let you inspect anything alone. If you ask, *"Can you show me the areas of the house that will need a lot of repairs?"* they will unlock and show you rooms that need repair, but they likely won't show you the worst rooms of the house. And if you say, *"Can you show me the rooms with the best views?"* You will most certainly be taken to the best rooms.

Most behavioral questions are written to do exactly what is described above. They signal which direction the candidate should go and create an environment in which they have too much control over what you will learn about them. The candidate will only take you to places that make them look good, bad places that are only relatively bad, or to places that don't exist.

The challenge you face as an interviewer is that the questions you ask must be specific enough to explain the topic you are trying to learn about, but not so specific that they provide signals to the correct answer.

Let's return to the house inspection analogy. Instead of the owner leading you on a tour, you want possession of the keys and the control to go where you want with the owner by your side. You want to be able to say, *"Let's look at the bedrooms. I'd like to start by looking inside the master bedroom."* Once you've inspected the master bedroom, you want to be able to say, *"Now I'm going to look inside the closet. Tell me about that hole in the wall? Thank you, now let's enter the bathroom. Are the tiles ceramic or porcelain?"*

This second experience has a completely different feel. You will uncover much more with this approach. To accomplish this with interview questions, you must remove any signals from the question about what the answer should be. For example, if the role you are hiring for operates in an unstructured environment, you could ask a traditional behavioral question:

> **Interviewer:** Give me an example of a time you successfully worked in an unstructured environment and had to move work forward without guidance.

This answer doesn't just signal what you want, it plainly tells the candidate you are looking for a person who can move work forward without guidance. If they haven't done this, they will create an answer—or more likely contort another answer they prepped in advance—to fit the question. Even if they wanted to give an honest answer showing how they struggled, this question specifically asks for an example of success. To take this from a leading question to an average question, make it as neutral as possible. Reduce the question to its core:

> **Interviewer:** Give me an example of a time you had to work in an unstructured environment.

There is still one problem with this question—it assumes the candidate has worked in an unstructured environment. What if they haven't? This question is improved but is still structured to force an answer out of the candidate. That isn't what you want. Instead make it more open-ended:

> **Interviewer:** Have you ever worked in an unstructured environment?

They will still sense that the "correct" answer is yes, but you have increased the odds of getting at the truth by allowing for an honest answer. With this open-ended question structure, there will be times when the candidate answers with the following:

> **Candidate:** I haven't had that experience yet, but I can share an example of an environment where things rarely went as planned, is that close enough?

That's exactly what you want. If you hadn't created the space for an honest answer, this candidate would have taken their example of an environment where things didn't go as planned and morphed it into an answer about an unstructured environment. Depending on their skill at "on-the-spot answer-morphing," you may or may not have gotten an answer that led to an accurate assessment. Since answer-morphing is not the skill you are assessing, make questions as signal-free as possible. That allows you to judge if the actual experience they've had is relevant.

Some questions are already relatively neutral. For example:

> **Interviewer:** Tell me about a time you needed information from a person who wasn't responsive. How did you manage that situation?

There isn't a lot to remove in this question and the candidate will know you are assessing their ability to work with people who may not be responsive. So, simply remove the assumption that the candidate has done what is being asked:

> **Interviewer:** Have you had an experience where you needed information from a person who wasn't responsive?

Both versions give some level of signal to the candidate about the answer being sought. But the second version gives the candidate more room to be honest, which improves the odds of learning the truth.

PRACTICE:
EQUAL CHOICES

Rather than reduce signals, another approach is to use a question structure that goes in the opposite direction and gives competing signals. The key to this design is to ask candidates a question and *have them choose between two answers that seem equally correct*. With this type of question there is no "right" answer and regardless of the candidate's response, it will reveal valuable insight on their thinking.

For example, if you wanted to assess "people management," you could ask the following:

> **Interviewer:** A person reporting to you has made an error in their work. Everyone on your team has been affected by it and is therefore aware of it. You have a one-hour meeting with your team (including the person who made the error) later that afternoon. Do you:
>
> - Use a portion of that meeting to briefly meet one-on-one with that person, discuss the error, and determine how to fix it so you can move forward quickly?
> - Use a portion of that meeting to briefly discuss the error with the full team and determine how to fix it so you can move forward quickly as a team?

The candidate has two choices: Both sound correct so there is no signal. Despite the best intentions of this structure, some candidates will still give an answer that lands in the middle:

> **Candidate:** I don't want to embarrass a person, respecting my team is important to me. But we can probably get to a great solution together as a team. Both options let me move forward quickly . . . . I'd probably talk to the person first, but then I'd discuss it immediately with the team with the person present. I'd probably identify one or two people from the team in advance and talk to them before I talked to the person who made the error, so I would know what I might be getting into and what some possible solutions are because as I think about it, I might not have the solution, the team might, so I can't just have the one guy making a solution, I need to incorporate the team. Yeah, that's what I would do . . .

This is a contrived answer and doesn't offer realistic actions someone would truly take. As a result, you still have no idea what this person would do and won't know what matters most to her. Does she prioritize not wanting to embarrass the person who made a mistake by having an individual feedback conversation? Or does she prioritize on-the-spot feedback and believes in modeling it in front of the team, so they get used to putting ego aside and moving forward?

To avoid this, incorporate a ranking element into the question. Ask the same question but use a scale with even numbers and have it written down, so you can show it to the candidate. It should look like this:

> A person reporting to you has made an error in their work. Everyone on your team has been affected by it and is therefore aware of it. You have a one-hour meeting with your team (including him) later that afternoon. On the scale below use the numbers to indicate in which direction you lean:

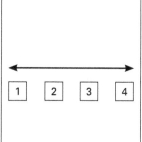

Using a set of even numbers forces them to pick a side. That is all you want to know—what side would they lean toward. Now you can have a real discussion to learn how they think by using any of these follow-up questions:

- Why do you lean in that direction?
- What are the pros and cons of that approach?
- Have you made a decision like this before?
- What did you learn from it?

To best assess this type of structure, you will have to know what works best in your culture. In the above example, do you want someone who cares more about preserving the reputation and confidence of their team member or cares more about creating an environment where open discussion and disagreement is the norm? Or, perhaps in your context neither end matters. Rather, you care more how they think, and your follow-up questions are then meant to better understand their thought process.

You have to be prepared for the candidate who still provides an answer that begins with "it depends":

Candidate: Well, it depends on the person. Ordinarily I would say just address it as a group, but if the person lacks confidence, I probably don't want to shut them down in front of people. That will demoralize them. Without knowing that, I can't really go one way or the other.

You can address this, and even benefit from it, by turning their "it depends" answer into your next follow-up question. By providing an "it depends" answer, the candidate has given you another set of options that you can make them choose from. Which in turn will reveal something about themselves. Your response to the above should be:

> **Interviewer:** Who do you have a harder time managing? Someone who lacks confidence like you just described? Or someone who is overconfident and could handle it in a group?
>
> **Candidate** (now a little unsure because they have to make a choice that reveals something about themselves . . .): Hmmm, if I had to choose . . . probably someone overconfident . . .
>
> **Interviewer:** Sounds good. Okay, so the person in this scenario is overconfident, on the scale of one to four, which direction do you lean?
>
> **Candidate:** Well, as I think about it, I'm probably a two on that one . . .

Now you know two things about the candidate.

- They have a harder time with people who lack confidence.
- They prefer to protect the reputation/confidence of their staff.

Here is another example of how to set up these types of questions.

> You need to gather some information quickly at work. You can go directly to the person with the information and ask for it.

But that person will likely need to ask their supervisor for permission first. You know neither the person nor their supervisor well. Use the scale below and choose the preferable approach.

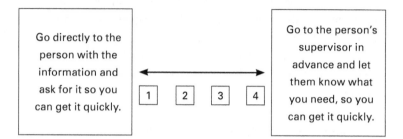

This question uncovers the candidate's view on hierarchy versus maintaining relationships and wanting to "go over their head." Once they've indicated which way they would lean, the follow up questions draw out the details:

- Why do you lean in that direction?
- What are the pros and cons of that approach?
- Have you made a decision like this before?
- What did you learn from it?

This design allows you to understand how people think. Nothing is foolproof, so always be prepared for an answer that tries to escape the structure. Don't get frustrated—use their answer to bring them back to the structure.

Candidate: My answer would depend on the culture of the org. Is this place very hierarchical?

Interviewer: I don't know, what's your preference as a manager, hierarchical or not?

Candidate: Hmmm . . . Hierarchy has its benefits, most places have some type of hierarchy.

> **Interviewer:** Okay, then then this place has a hierarchy. Which way do you lean . . . ?

> **Candidate:** Probably a two. Even in a hierarchy, I'd want to connect with that person first.

> **Interviewer:** Sounds good. Tell me a bit more about why that matters to you . . .

You still had to chase down their answer, but the structure allows you to learn more about them (e.g., you now know they prefer hierarchy).

You should expect an exchange like the one above and not be concerned. In this exchange, the candidate makes a good point—organizational culture and structure do matter. For a person who likes to think through things, this structure can feel rigid, so it is fine for you as the interviewer to have to clarify. But if that clarification goes into several exchanges back and forth, you are likely facing a candidate who has issues with ambiguity and making decisions. They are more concerned with being "right." They can't grasp that what is most important is their ability to choose and explain. You should flag this as a concern for follow up.

To be most effective, the Equal Choices structure should be created based on actual situations that have occurred in your organization. The interviewer will know the area of discussion well enough to be able to discern a strong answer from a weak one. You will have to create several of these types of questions in advance. It takes more work but is worth it. Once you've created a set of 5–10, you can use them indefinitely and you will realize you've made a one-time upfront investment that reduces interference across many interviews to come.

PART 2

PRESSURE MANAGEMENT

Interviewing well isn't easy. But it shouldn't be unnecessarily hard. What makes interviewing hard for candidates is pressure. There are two types of pressure the candidate feels: the type you apply as the interviewer and the type they put on themselves. The pressure you apply that leads to a better answer is necessary. The candidate's self-imposed pressure is unnecessary and gets in the way of accurate assessment.

There is also a pressure that you experience as the interviewer. This pressure shows up after the interview when you feel the need to make the right decision. Knowing how to release pressure, apply pressure, and make decisions under pressure will shift the odds in your favor.

TO END WITH TRUTH, START WITH TRUST

*E*very candidate enters the interview room with a degree of uncertainty about what to expect. They are about to sit across the table from someone who controls their future. Regardless of how confident or comfortable they seem, they have their guard up to protect themselves. The protection is necessary because each side wants something the other has, and neither is sure they want to give it up. The interviewer has a job they are holding for just the right person. The candidate holds the truth about who they truly are and what they can do. But they don't know if what they have is what is being sought. That pressure makes the candidate not sure how much of themselves they should reveal.

The power dynamic in the room doesn't help. Since the interviewer is asking all the questions, he also has all the answers. The interviewer is perfect and has the power. The candidate has something to prove and feels judged. It is a dynamic in which interviewer and candidate are not equals and adds to the pressure.

From the first moments of the interview, you must create an environment that allows the candidate to willingly reveal their true selves. Lowering the pressure will get them to lower their guard. To do so, make three things clear:

- You and the candidate are equals.

- You and the candidate are working toward an outcome together.
- It is in both of your best interests to be open and honest.

These three bullets describe an interview utopia you may never reach. The modern definition of an interview is strongly imprinted in every candidate's mind. The candidate's desire to avoid giving the wrong answer and to get the job is part of this entrenched perception. But you don't need utopia. What you need is to increase the chance of getting an accurate assessment. Every practice that brings down their guard, even slightly, achieves that goal.

PRACTICE:
MINIMIZE PHYSICAL BARRIERS

In any training on effective public presentations, you will always learn about the importance of stepping from behind the podium or stepping toward the audience to increase connection. The same holds true for interviewing. If there is a physical barrier between you and the candidate, you must minimize it to increase a feeling of equality.

In most interviews, you are behind a desk or a table. Don't stay seated. Break the barrier. Step from behind the desk or table to shake hands and introduce yourself. The message you are sending is that you are equals standing on the same ground with nothing between you. Make sure there is water in the room. Ask if they would like some. And pour it for them. The message again is clear, "I'm not above you. I'm here to help."

Next, call attention to the fact that there is a physical barrier between the two of you.

Interviewer: Good morning. Thanks for joining us today.

Candidate: Happy to be here, thanks for having me.

Interviewer: I usually don't like to have such a big space between me and someone I'm interested in learning more about, but we'll do our best to make this work.

The message you are sending is that despite the barrier, you are still on the same side. Their guard isn't completely down yet, but it's dropped an inch or two.

PRACTICE:
COMMON POINTS

Research shows people trust someone if they feel they have something in common with them.[1] Your goal is finding something you and the candidate have in common to build that initial reserve of trust. Many interviewers review the resume through the assessment lens only and focus their attention solely on titles, responsibilities, accomplishments, etc. You must also look for other things that allow you to find initial points of commonality.

Research shows people trust
someone if they feel they have
something in common with them.

A great place to start is by finding an item listed on their resume that isn't directly work-related but should be easy for the candidate to talk about:

- Where they currently live
- The cities in which they have worked
- Where they went to school
- Their major

- Items listed in the Miscellaneous/Other section
  - A hobby or language you are familiar with
  - A sport they were a part of that interests you
  - Volunteer work that you are familiar with or completely unfamiliar with

This is how you may discover that you both lived or worked in the same city at some point. Perhaps you and the candidate have a school in common. In the miscellaneous section you may find a common interest or language. Or you may find something that genuinely interests you. The idea is for you to continue a normal conversation that gets them to put their guard down a little more. That way, when it eventually does come back up—it always does—it isn't as high.

> **Interviewer:** I noticed you used to work in Wisconsin. My grandmother lives there.
>
> **Candidate:** Really, what part?
>
> **Interviewer:** Just outside Madison, small town. You familiar with that area?
>
> **Candidate:** Yup, loved it, not the winter though, but really enjoyed my time there.
>
> **Interviewer:** Did you ever go to the summer festival?

There are some candidates for whom this won't work because they prefer to stay purely professional during interviews. In those cases, this approach can backfire.

> **Interviewer:** I noticed you used to work in Wisconsin. My grandmother lives there.
>
> **Candidate:** I haven't been back in a while.

Interviewer: She lived just outside Madison, small town. You familiar with that area?

Candidate: No, not really.

Interviewer: Did you ever go to the summer festival? I loved it when I was a kid . . .

Candidate: Oh, okay.

That conversation isn't going anywhere and just feels awkward. That defeats the purpose of putting the candidate at ease. The sooner you can pick up on this, the sooner you can transition to the interview questions because they are likely more comfortable addressing those.*

A word of caution on finding points of commonality. They can lead to bias. If you only find something in common with some of the candidates, there is potential for you to also feel more connected to those candidates. You may then view them more favorably than candidates for whom you did not find a point of commonality. Consistency is again a critical element. If you are going to use this approach you absolutely must do it for every candidate. This isn't always easy, but if you take the time there is always something on a candidate's resume that rings familiar and that is what you use to build trust.

PRACTICE:
SET EXPECTATIONS OF "WE"

At this point you've addressed physical barriers and found a point of commonality. Before diving into the interview, take one more minute to set expectations that let the candidate view you as someone on their

---

* If any portion of your evaluation rests on the candidate's ability to connect interpersonally, then you should note their difficulty with this approach as a potential issue to further assess.

side rather than an adversary. It must be clear that your job is to make sure the two of you make the correct decision regarding their future with your organization. The message you are sending is that you are working on their behalf and it benefits them to be as open as possible with you.

This only works if the candidate believes you. They must believe that you want what is best for them. For this to work, you must genuinely want what is best for them. You can't just say the words. Your belief that you are there to help them must drive this approach.

Don't beat around the bush when setting the expectations. Clearly articulate that this is a partnership to reach a common goal. A "partnership" will not be how they are accustomed to viewing the interviewer/candidate relationship: Your words will shift that, even if only slightly.

> **Interviewer:** Well, at some point hopefully we'll get a chance to talk more about Wisconsin. For now, let me give you a sense of what to expect over the next hour or so.
>
> **Candidate:** That would be great.
>
> **Interviewer:** During this interview I want to learn about you. I also want to help you understand this organization because you are also making a decision. I will answer any questions you have to help with that decision. We're both here to learn and are in this together. Our goal should be for each of us to better understand the other. All right, let's start by talking about your experience with . . .

In the example, the interviewer is being blunt about what they want for the candidate. But they are also modeling openness and a willingness to share. The interviewer is showing that she is there to help the candidate. The words "we," "our," and "together" must be in this preamble. The second to last line is critical and some version of it should also always be included. It clearly states the goal—and the goal isn't to get the job. The goal is to understand each other.

The candidate may not entirely agree with that goal, but that is fine. By this point, you've removed physical barriers, created equal footing, modeled openness, and positioned yourself as someone who can help. In total, this has taken less than five minutes. The candidate will be a bit more relaxed. You have successfully moved them from where they were when they entered with their guard up. Their guard is now lowered and the probability of finding the truth has been raised.

YOU'RE NOT ASSESSING THE CANDIDATE. THEY'RE ASSESSING THEMSELVES.

*T*he accepted belief about interviews is that you, the interviewer, are assessing the candidate. This belief is so integral to the definition of an interview that other explanations don't seem plausible. Any belief so engrained that it isn't questioned, needs to be disrupted.

During an interview you are the one asking the questions. So far so good. But when you analyze what happens next, the belief falls apart. The first thing the candidate does in response to a question is delve into their brain, selecting from a range of experiences, perspectives, and opinions. When they come back out, they share what they found. You then ask them what they did well, what they could have done better, and what they would do differently next time.

None of this is you assessing the candidate. What you have just done is ask the candidate to retrieve a memory and assess it themselves. You are judging the quality and relevance of their self-assessment.

When you tilt the interview to look at it from this angle, you expose two problems. First, interviews rely entirely on the candidate's ability to accurately recall events, results, and decisions. Second, your assessment relies on their ability to evaluate themselves.

Science suggests those are big problems. Countless studies show that stress negatively impacts working memory.[1] The type of stress that most impacts memory is psychosocial stress. In other words, stress from interacting with people—like during an interview. In cognitive psychology, working memory refers to the function of the brain that allows the explanation of stored information—like during an interview.

It gets worse. As they are sharing their memory, the candidate needs to evaluate it and tell you how well they did or didn't do. Once again, science is not on our side. Research shows self-evaluation is inherently difficult.[2] People often have the wrong view of their own competence because they don't have enough subjective information to accurately self-assess.

So, not only are we asking candidates to remember something under sub-optimal conditions, we are also asking them to do something humans aren't good at doing.

Now that we see the interview in a different light, let's bring science back on our side, remove unnecessary pressure, and improve the odds. First, we'll address the issue of memory. Then we'll share several practices that make it easier for the candidate to self-assess and for you to discover the truth.

PRACTICE:
THE MEMORY ANCHOR

Many interviewers hold the opinion that the candidate should know their resume front to back. An interviewer once told me, "A candidate shouldn't need their resume in front of them to answer my questions. If they aren't prepared, they don't meet the bar." That type of faulty thinking is why organizations lose out on great talent. Candidates who don't need their resume in front of them are great interviewees. But you are not looking for a great interviewee. You are looking for someone who can excel at the job you are hiring for.

You do want the candidate to be prepared and know what they've done. You rarely need someone with the memory of a blackjack card-counter who can pull facts and stats out of thin air on command. A memorized resume is an impressive party trick, but unless that ability is aligned to a skill you are looking for, it isn't what you should be assessing for.

My preference is for the truth. The truth isn't memorized. It isn't rehearsed. The truth is the answer that comes out of the candidate with very little energy spent on them trying to recollect what happened. The truth comes from them *reflecting* on what happened. To lower the memory hurdle, you should intentionally use the resume as a "memory anchor."

The truth isn't memorized. It isn't rehearsed. The truth is the answer that comes out of the candidate with very little energy spent on them trying to recollect what happened. The truth comes from them reflecting on what happened.

This is different than the strict "Resume Interview" which is a type of interview we'll discuss in the next chapter. The Memory Anchor protocol is simply the following:

- At the start of the interview, ask the candidate if they have their resume.
- If they do, ask them to pull it out and feel free to use it to help answer any question.
- If they don't have their resume, provide them a copy.

Your job is to lower the psychosocial stress of interviewing and *help* the candidate access their thoughts. You want them to reflect on those thoughts and give you enough insight to help with your ultimate decision. The resume as an anchor solves the first part. Now let's combine that with how to improve their self-assessment, which we'll tackle next.

SOCIAL COMPARISON THEORY

Dr. Leon Festinger is a social psychologist recognized for developing multiple concepts which have shaped our understanding of human behavior. Theories such as "cognitive dissonance" and "the proximity effect" originated from his research at MIT, the University of Michigan, the University of Minnesota, and Stanford University. During this time he also developed the theory that people intrinsically want accurate self-assessments. His research found we accomplish this by comparing ourselves to others. Because we are unclear on how to judge ourselves, we rely on comparison to reduce uncertainty in the areas we lack information. This discovery came to be known as Social Comparison Theory.

Most interview questions that attempt to determine a candidate's skill rely on the candidate sharing a prepared answer that begins with, "My strengths are . . ." followed at some point by, "My development areas are . . ." This is an example of a self-assessment that the candidate was ready to give. Your follow-up questions are your only tool to determine if you can take their word for it. But a strong candidate, having anticipated this, will be equipped with examples as evidence.

To distinguish between someone who is just a strong candidate and someone who will be a strong hire, you instead want them to reflect in real-time, so you can observe how they've come to view their strengths and gaps as such. The fundamental human impulse to compare is the perfect mechanism for this type of reflection. The next two practices leverage this impulse and accurately identify a candidate's skills and development areas. In both practices, the resume serves as the anchor and a set of comparison-based questions leads to an unrehearsed truth with increased depth and context.

PRACTICE:
COMPARISON ACROSS TIME

No one likes to be the object of comparison if they won't fare well. To circumvent that issue, use a set of questions that compare the candidate to the one person they are least likely to resist being compared to—themselves. The questions are asked in a specific order and the practice is structured as follows:

> **Interviewer:** Take a look at your resume and find a role or project you had three or four years ago. Describe for me the skills you needed back then to succeed at work.

> **Candidate:** Sure . . . when I was VP at GoTech International, I needed strong analytical skills, written communication was also important, and project planning. Those were important because . . .

This first question establishes a baseline. It is the comparison point. Now follow with the second question in the series:

> **Interviewer:** Now let's think about you today. Of the skills you just listed, which ones do you still use frequently now?

> **Candidate:** Project planning is still something I use constantly, analysis as well . . . . I do far less writing now . . .

This pair of questions uncovers potential strengths. In this example, project planning and analysis. They are strengths for one of two reasons. Either because the candidate's job has required him to exercise those skills for at least three to four years. Or, because the candidate plays to his own strengths and these are the ones he continued to rely on to succeed. Either way, you now have context that matters because strengths develop over time.*

---

* On rare occasions a candidate's current skills will have no overlap with skills from three to four years ago. If so, that is fine. A list of skills they've leveraged and the context in which they used them is still valuable for follow-up.

Now follow with a third question that continues to leverage comparison:

> **Interviewer:** What skills do you have currently that you didn't have three to four years ago?
>
> **Candidate:** Hmmm, I manage people now, so people management. I also work across departments much more, so relationship-building . . .

This stage of the questions uncovers growth as exhibited by additional skill acquisition. They should be able to list skills they didn't mention before. A concerning answer is if they don't have any new skills or they simply *know* more now. For example:

> **Candidate:** Well, I am much stronger now at those same skills. And I just understand so much more about the industry than I did back then. I also have more relationships.

There is nothing wrong with having more knowledge, but *everyone* should know more after several years. New skill development is the higher bar for differentiating high performers. If the candidate has stayed in the same role it is possible they may not have developed *new* skills. In that case demonstration of *stronger* skills is a valid answer. If you need a strong performer in a specific area, and you don't anticipate your role evolving, then an answer indicating stronger skills is perfectly acceptable.

Having said that, I don't know many roles that have stayed the same in the last five years nor will stay the same in the next five. Part of what defines high performers is their ability to get stronger at what they do *while also* developing new skills. When I don't see new skill development, I note it as a concern.

The final question in this quartet again uses comparison to provide context:

Interviewer: Now let's look to the future. What skills would you like to have in three to four years that you don't have now?

Candidate: Great question. I don't understand the financial side of this work as much as I'd like, so it would be great to get some exposure to that. Also, I'm just now starting to manage large teams of managers, each with their own large teams . . .

This question highlights their development areas. If any skill they share is a primary aspect of the work you need done, you now have areas to explore in subsequent interviews.

The rhythm of these questions, in which the candidate reflects and compares herself only to herself, keeps her in a positive frame of mind. This allows you to get more honest information than if the question pushed her into a defensive position. It isn't until the last question, where she acknowledges there are things she can't do now, that tension may arise.

Most people will recognize that this last question is about development areas. But by this point the structure of the previous questions makes the progression feel fair and natural and you'll find that candidates answer thoughtfully and willingly.

Evasive Answers

Occasionally candidates will resist giving a straight answer to the last question and will become evasive. This means you will have to be more direct with your follow-up questions:

Candidate: That's a tough one, since I'm not sure exactly what my role will look like five years from now it's hard for me to say what skills I'd like to have

Interviewer: Let's think about it differently then. Of the skills you've discussed so far, which ones do you want to improve over the next five years?

If a candidate continues to avoid these answers, that raises a flag for you. It indicates a candidate who doesn't have the ability to reflect or doesn't possess the honesty to discuss an area they want to improve.

Career Length

The length of a candidate's career is important to keep in mind with this protocol. Their career length can serve as a valid explanation for why a candidate may not have new skills to share. If a person describes skills from several years ago, and they have five to ten years of work experience, they should show skill development. But if five years ago, they were already twenty years into their career, then new skill development may be harder to come by.

For candidates with more than fifteen years of experience you can avoid this by using the same set of comparison questions, but structure the wording of the first question differently:

> **Interviewer:** Take a look at your resume and think about the various roles you had during the first ten years of your career . . . . Describe the skills you needed back then to do well during that phase of your career.

With this adjustment the remainder of the questions still allow you to identify skill progression and potentially growth.

The candidate's answers during this protocol will generate a set of strengths as well as areas where they need to improve. This allows you to compare that list with your hiring criteria and decide whether the candidate can be developed in the areas that don't meet your bar.

PRACTICE:
GIVE THEM BRAGGING RIGHTS

High performers all have moments when they realize they are stronger than others in certain areas. Either they have been explicitly recognized for a set of skills or they became the "go-to" person for specific projects. You want to help them access those memories. This leads to a different type of comparison question in which candidates contextualize their skill by comparing themselves to co-workers.

High performers all have moments when they realize they are stronger than others in certain areas.

This protocol lets you learn their strengths more effectively than a rehearsed "My strengths are . . ." answer. But it also feels unnatural to the candidate to blatantly brag. This is framed at the outset to address that tension:

> **Interviewer:** Look at your resume and find a few examples of something you were able to do better than those around you at the time . . . . This isn't a trick question, I'm not trying to figure out if you are humble. Just share with me some experiences when you had that realization . . .

Be direct about the fact that you aren't looking for humility. Candidates always try to decipher the purpose of a question. It is an accepted part of interview culture. It is also a waste of mental effort and blocks the truth. Your initial acknowledgment that you know what they may be thinking makes it okay for them to not be humble.

> **Candidate:** Well . . . a few years ago we had a project in Brazil, working with a company we had recently acquired. The employees of this company spoke decent English, so that wasn't the issue, the problem was they did not trust any of us from the parent company. Not one bit. On that project, I turned out to be the one that could really gain their trust and get them to open up, share information, and begin to see us as partners . . .

To increase your confidence that you've found a true strength, gather context about results with the second question:

> **Interviewer:** What results did this lead to?

> **Candidate:** Other people on my team struggled with working across cultures and making bonds. The work under them just stagnated. I became the guy who managed five of the cross-team projects in Brazil . . .

If you had started this series of questions without the explanatory preamble, it would be hard for them to get going. Once you've eased them into the comparison framework, it allows their mind to follow that path more naturally. You can now repeat the same set of questions once more to bring out other skills.

> **Interviewer:** Do you have another instance where you realized you were stronger than someone else? . . . What results did this lead to?

Development Areas

Once you've identified a few strengths, shift gears. After letting them speak highly of themselves you can ask a question they will feel obligated to answer honestly.

> **Interviewer:** Now, take a look at your resume and tell me about a few experiences when you had to go to someone else for help because they were stronger in a certain area?

The order of the questions normalizes the idea that some people are better than others in certain areas. No one is perfect. We all have growth areas and turn to others for help. By the time you ask this question, the candidate is primed to share a development area. The structure minimizes feelings of judgment that get in the way of vulnerability. Some candidates will try to equivocate and justify their answer:

> **Candidate:** Well this other guy had been around way longer than me . . . so of course he was better at this than me . . . .

Their attempts to justify don't matter. Let them keep talking and you'll still uncover an area that needs growth.

Questions with comparison as the engine are powerful because we have all had experiences where we realized our strengths or recognized strength in others. Helping a candidate access those moments in which they've said to themselves, *"I'm good at this,"* or *"She's better than me at this,"* provides a better self-assessment. Your personality and style will determine whether you prefer the candidate to draw comparisons to themselves or to others. Try out both and you'll quickly determine which works best for you.

PRESSURE CLARIFIES AND REVEALS POTENTIAL

*S*trategies 4 and 5 reduce the types of pressure that negatively impact your ability to learn more about the candidate during the interview. Minimizing pressure is good when it leads to better insight and more accurate decisionmaking. Pressure, however, also has its benefits.

In other fields, such as chemistry and physics, pressure is intentionally applied because of its ability to clarify and reveal potential. In the scientific context, the cliché "pressure makes diamonds" isn't cliché. Carbon is commonly used for graphite in pencil leads. But under extreme pressure, it forms diamonds. Oxygen is normally a colorless gas. Under pressure it not only becomes solid, but turns bright red. Sulfur, an ingredient in matches and fireworks, was recently discovered to be an electrical superconductor when exposed to high pressure.

The positive and negative impact of pressure on human behavior has likewise been deeply researched. A considerable amount of the studies have been done in the fields of sports, law enforcement, the military, student performance, and leadership. In all fields there is a point when pressure goes from enhancing performance to hindering it. But that tipping point varies across people and settings. What is consistent is the finding that pressure which challenges people is helpful, and pressure that threatens is not.

Dr. Martin Turner, psychology professor and lecturer on performance, describes the challenge state as, "a positive mental approach to pressure situations where our mental resources meet the demands of the situation."[1] The threat state is the opposite and decreases the ability to focus and make decisions. Dr. Hendrie Weisinger, author of the bestselling book *Performing Under Pressure: The Science of Doing Your Best When It Matters Most*, explains the benefit of being challenged as, "individuals who perceive a task or situation not as a threat but instead as a challenge, an opportunity, or fun are far more likely to perform up to the level of their ability, increasing their chances for success."[2]

As an interviewer your goal is not to apply extreme pressure, nor do you need to know each candidate's tipping point for optimal performance. You need to know how to appropriately challenge candidates to gain insight for an accurate assessment. While you do want to apply pressure that clarifies and reveals potential, this is neither chemistry nor psychics—you don't want to change their state of being. You want to understand their state of being. How you apply pressure that challenges candidates depends on the type of insight you are pursuing. If you need specifics, that requires one type of pressure. If you just want more information, that leads to a different approach. Let's learn how to do both.

PRACTICE:
KEEP QUESTIONS LEAN AND FOLLOW-UPS SPECIFIC

Whenever you ask questions during an interview, you inevitably will get an answer that does not provide the information you need to help make a decision. There are a range of reasons for this—none of them should have anything to do with your questions themselves. Strategy 3 showed how to remove signals from a question. A rule of thumb to accompany that strategy is:

1. Keep the question as short as possible
2. Keep it open-ended and use specific follow-up questions

Keeping the question short and open-ended puts you in stronger position of control. Not only because of less signals but because once the candidate starts talking, the follow-up questions can be targeted to gather specific and relevant information. The follow up questions should help you learn the following:

- Their thought processes
  - What made you think/do/believe that?
- Whether they got results, and why or why not
  - What results did that lead to? Why?
- Whether they adapt and grow
  - How have you grown since then? What advice would you give your former self?

These questions are a level of challenge that most interviewers anticipate and are prepared for. But using these rules doesn't always lead to helpful answers. Sometimes candidates pick an example that doesn't illuminate what you need to know, or they don't explain it well, or they give a rehearsed answer. In those instances, you need to apply pressure that challenges them more and follow a third rule:

3. When necessary, tell the candidate what was wrong with the way they answered.

The following are ways to frame a follow-up question to gain clarity:

- That answer was very general, I could use some more specifics to help me understand.

4. I'm not clear on what role you played and what you accomplished in that example.

- I don't understand what the goal of that project was and whether you got there.

This should then be followed by:

- Can you give me a better answer than that?

Put together, your follow-up question could be . . .

- I'm not clear on what role you played and what you accomplished in that example. Can you give me a better answer than that?

Or it could be . . .

- That answer was very general, I could use some more specifics to help me understand. Can you give me a better answer than that?

This type of follow-up question requires you to be blunt and honest. Depending on your style, it may feel rude to be that direct. Keep in mind that is only your perception. Your tone in asking the question is factual, not aggressive. Think of yourself as giving the candidate an opportunity to get better. If they are strong in the areas you need them to be, they will respond with stronger answers. If that approach isn't your nature, then it is even more important to be prepared to apply pressure with this type of question when needed. If you don't challenge them, you'll lose opportunities to get closer to the truth.

PRACTICE:
LET IT BREATHE

Within the CIA there is an entity called the Center for the Study of Intelligence (CSI). This group manages classified and unclassified materials on the history and methodology of intelligence gathering. The CSI publishes *Studies in Intelligence*, a quarterly peer-reviewed academic journal. In the archives of this journal lives an article explaining interview tactics used by investigators to break a suspect without physically breaking them.[3] The approaches include various types of psychological pressure, and the majority do not apply to the process of interviewing candidates, except for one—the use of silence to gain more information.

As job interviewers, we've been conditioned to associate interviewing with questioning, conversation, and interaction. We rarely think of the opposite. Of all the weapons in the interviewer's arsenal, silence is an underutilized one. It's not just the CIA that knows this. Some of the most famous interviewers of our time use silence as a tactic and make no secret of it. Famed talk show host Dick Cavett often interviewed celebrities who were hesitant to provide details of a story. In those moments, Cavett used an approach he described as, "holding someone with silence and making them go on." He would simply pause after an answer was given and leave a long empty space. The person across the table would invariably begin to say things they were not planning to share.

> Of all the weapons in the
> interviewer's arsenal, silence
> is an underutilized one.

News anchor and political debate moderator Jim Lehrer has similar advice for interviewers:

> If you resist the temptation to respond too quickly to the answer, you'll discover something almost magical. The other person will either expand on what he's already said, or he'll go in a different direction. Either way, he's expanding his response, and you get a clear view into his head and heart.

As an interviewer, you should strategically use silence when interviewing a candidate. When you ask an initial question, sometimes you need to rephrase it for clarity. But when asking any follow-up question after that, let it hang between the two of you. Resist the urge to fill that silence. Train yourself to mentally count to five. The silence is a challenge that will draw in the candidate. It is a vacuum that pulls at whatever is in their heart and mind.

Five seconds will feel like an eternity and takes practice because most of us are uncomfortable with silence. Use that to your advantage. Counting puts you in control during the pause. Meanwhile the candidate isn't sure how to interpret it. Let them give in to that desire to end discomfort. If they don't talk, then you can move on to the next question. Odds are, they will talk. The more they talk, the more information you are gathering. More importantly, that information will be increasingly unrehearsed.

Improved Executive Function

There is more to this technique than simply hoping pressure makes the candidate fill open space with something useful. Part of the practice is to help the candidate fill that space with deeper insight you wouldn't normally get. Science tells us that silence helps with that as well, because it actually improves how the brain operates.

A study at the University of Pavia in Italy was conducted to learn more about how music makes the brain relax.[4] During the experiment, researchers played different types of music and measured the psychological and physiological impact. What they learned about silence happened quite by accident. There were short pauses between the musical tracks, during which the metrics continued to be measured. They found that music did relax the brain, but to everyone's surprise what relaxed the brain more than anything was the silence between the musical tracks.

During an interview, candidates use the part of their brain called the prefrontal cortex. This is known as executive function and controls the ability to differentiate among conflicting thoughts, determine good and bad, better and best, future consequences of current activities, and prediction of outcomes. These are exactly the types of self-assessment you want from the candidate. Ceaseless questions can drain this part of the brain and lead to less insight. Silence relaxes the mind and restores those cognitive resources.

To get the most useful information out of a candidate, you can't pound them with question after question. You need to provide their brain with restorative pauses. Use silence specifically after the candidate has provided an answer that was too shallow or not quite what you needed. After they complete their answer, say nothing. Let it take on a life of its own. If you don't let the question breathe, the answer will die. If you talk, you are filling that silence with information for them to process. Instead, get out of the way so they can fill the void with a moment of restoration, then reflection, and then more information. The silence compels them to dig deeper. To step up to the challenge. The truth that tumbles out is more insightful and purer than anything you could have said to elicit an answer.

To get the most useful information out of a candidate, you can't pound them with question after question. You need to provide their brain with restorative pauses.

STOP RATIONALIZING

*T*he reason to hire a candidate is because they are the best person for the job. But after completing a candidate's interview process, there are pressures that can influence you to hire them when perhaps you shouldn't. You may feel pressure to fill the position because it has been open longer than intended. You may feel pressure because the candidate had an average interview but was better than other candidates and you're concerned you won't find someone stronger. The pressure to hire may occur because it takes a lot of work to interview candidates, and you don't have capacity to continue interviewing. Think of a hiring mistake you've made, and you can likely recall moments during their interview process that indicated it wouldn't end well, but you pressed forward and hired the candidate anyway. Whatever the pressure, at the core of this faulty decisionmaking is our brain's ability to rationalize.

In psychology, rationalization is a defense mechanism in which questionable decisions are justified in a logical manner to make them tolerable. Rationalization preys on two powerful parts of human nature, our wants and our desire to feel good. We rationalize because we want something, and we want to feel good about it. Since we don't have to deal with the repercussions in the moment, we convince ourselves they may not happen and it is worth the risk. Rationalization helps reduce cognitive dissonance, an uncomfortable psychological state produced by discrepancies between actions and attitudes.[1] When we later acknowledge the mistake and say, "hindsight is twenty-twenty," we are still protecting our egos. It isn't that our hindsight is better, it's that we are now dealing with the repercussions we anticipated and can no longer deny it.

The key to conquering this self-deception is understanding that in the moment—when we make mistakes that we need to rationalize—*we know we are making a mistake*. That's precisely why we rationalize. Rationalizing requires your brain to first recognize you are being irrational—only then does it begin the process of justifying. That moment of recognition is what strong interviewers learn to identify and control.

PRACTICE:
PREMORTEM

The trick is to have the same clarity of thought *during* the decision as you will *after* the decision. It can be difficult to discern between when you are rationalizing and when you are just making a good case for the candidate by weighing the pros and cons. In those moments, when you are leaning toward hiring a candidate, potentially against your best judgement, conduct what cognitive psychologist Dr. Gary Klein calls a "premortem" before making a final decision.[2]

Conducting a premortem will feel like a counterintuitive approach because rather than envisioning success with this candidate, you envision failure. Imagine hiring the candidate and then imagine every concern you have the candidate becoming true. Imagine all the bad ways this will play out. The deadlines they will miss. The relationships they will damage. The decrease in team productivity. Imagine firing them because of what you knew during the interview. Imagine having to restart the hiring process.

To resist the tremendous power of rationalization, you need a power just as equal. The power of your imagination fits the bill. It allows you to imagine what your twenty-twenty hindsight might be. This mental exercise taps into that power and takes you out of the moment when temptation is strong. Articulating what could go wrong brings you back from the brink of doing what you want and forces you to think more clearly about what you need. You may still decide to hire the candidate. But if you do, you've shifted the odds toward it being the rational decision versus the one you rationalized.

PART 3

SHARP TOOLS

Like a physician, the interviewer's job is to diagnose. Physicians use a structured process of question, answer, and examination to gather insight. When the issue is complex, they draw blood. An interviewer's job, to delve into the candidate's mind, is complex. It also requires them to draw from the candidate. But not blood. Answers.

The interviewer's tools must be as sharp as any physician's instruments. The tools must be clean so as not to pollute the answer. The interviewer must know which tools to use when and what to look for in the answer they've drawn.

AN INTERVIEW
IS A GLIMPSE

*T*his book is about changing the way you think about interviews. It is about redefining what an interview is. It is worth asking, then, what is this tool we call an interview? A quick review of several dictionaries reveals an interesting pattern:

> *Merriam-Webster:* n. a formal consultation usually to evaluate qualifications (as of a prospective student or employee)

> *Cambridge Dictionary:* n. a formal meeting at which a person who is interested in getting a job or other position is asked questions to learn how well the person would be able to do it

> *Oxford Dictionary:* v. to question (someone) to discover their opinions or experience • to orally examine (an applicant for a job, college admission, etc.)

The modern meaning of *interview* is tightly associated with assessing talent. As a result, these definitions provide little additional insight beyond what we already know. Let's put those definitions aside and look to the original meaning of the word from the sixteenth century. The Middle French origin of "interview" is:

entrevue, derived from *s'entrevoir,* to see each other, visit each other briefly, have a glimpse of

This definition is untainted by the modern experience of job interviewing—one which we've established as flawed and ineffective. The word *s'entrevoir* provides greater insight. An interview is people spending time together, a visit. It is not a one-sided event in which the interviewer has all the power and control: It is an interaction, with each side seeing and influencing the other along the way. Philosophically, much of what we've covered so far aligns with this definition. What adds to the complexity is the second half of the Middle French version—an interview is brief. It is only a glimpse of someone else.

The brevity of the interaction points toward two things. First, use the time well. Leave nothing to chance. If something is only working 50 percent of the time, then strip it down, keep what works, and rethink what doesn't. Second, to get a full picture of the candidate, take each glimpse from a very different angle.

The following practices do just that. They are a reexamination of common interviews. You will find a reimagining of the phone interview. A refinement of the resume interview. A reworking of the behavioral interview. And a reminder of why you should never interview alone. They are a sharpened set of tools. Each provides a glimpse from an alternate vantage point.

PRACTICE:
THE REVERSE INTERVIEW

Once you begin reviewing the resumes of candidates interested in your role, you'll be able to cut candidates simply based on what you see on paper. At that point, you may feel you are ready to advance some of the candidates to an in-person interview. But a candidate who looks strong on paper doesn't always turn out the same in person. By the time you realize that, you've already invested several hours interviewing the candidate live. You can gain some of the same insight and save time by spending twenty minutes conducting a phone screen.

When I first began interviewing, I did traditional phone screens asking the following questions:

- How did you learn about this role?
- What interests you in the role?
- What interests you in the organization?
- Why are you considering leaving your current role?
- A clarifying question or two about their resume, e.g.:
  - It looks like your last two positions overlapped, am I reading that correctly?

Even though phone screens saved time in the long run, doing them well still took too much time out of my day. I wasn't feeling the payoff. The call was about thirty minutes, but preparing for the call, reviewing their resume, making sure my questions were relevant, and thinking of additional questions to ask added another fifteen to twenty minutes.

At the end of any phone screen, if I planned to advance the candidate, I gave them time to ask questions about the role or organization. Even if I wasn't planning on advancing them, out of respect, I still gave them a few minutes to ask questions. There were times when a strong candidate lost ground because of the weakness of questions they asked. This was often a signal of things to come. On the other hand, there were weaker candidates who turned things around by the strength of their questions and ended up doing well in the remainder of the interview process.

I reflected on what I was trying to learn about the candidate during the phone screen and it boiled down to four basic pieces of information:

- Do they communicate well?
- Have they done research on our organization?
- Why are they interested in the role?
- Clarifications based on their resume

I realized the reason candidates gained or lost ground with me during their Q&A portion of the call was because I was learning as much, if not more, about these four areas from the questions they asked me than from the questions I asked them. I decided to add a twist to the phone screen and created The Reverse Phone Screen.

THE STRUCTURE

The Reverse Screen is simple, and its structure is designed to make easy, accurate cuts. It turns the tables and gives the candidate ten to fifteen minutes to ask the interviewer the top ten questions they have about the role, the organization, etc. The interviewer then takes five to ten minutes to ask the candidate a few questions. With this flipped structure, the questions that candidates ask and how well they prepare tell me a ton about them, yet my preparation is minimal.

To make this work, notify the candidate in advance via email of the reversed structure. This gives them time to prepare. For example:

> Thank you for your interest in our organization. The first step in our process is a phone screen. We do our phone screens slightly differently than most organizations. The call will last 20 to 25 minutes and during the first 10 to 15 minutes, you will be asking the questions. Be prepared to ask up to 10 questions that are important to you. They can be about the role, the team, the organization or any other facet of this opportunity. We will then take 5 to 10 minutes to ask you follow-up questions if necessary.

The Reverse Screen is a great way to save time and energy. It changes the flow of the discussion so it is less one-sided, allowing it to be more natural and give you a chance to gain great insight. You can easily assess some key basics:

- Have they researched the organization?
  - If they ask very basic questions that could have been answered by perusing your website, then they haven't researched your organization.

- If they ask strong questions based on something they read about your organization, then they have researched your organization.
- What matters to them? What interests them?
  - If they ask questions about the vision, the plan for the next five years, or anything that helps them understand the strategic side of the work and how their role fits in, those are great questions.
  - If they ask questions about culture, the manager's style, and how performance is measured, those are also great questions.
  - If their questions are more weighted toward asking about work hours, the amount of travel required, or benefits, that is a bad sign. Those things matter, but if the candidate leads with those, they are likely just looking for a job, not looking to work for your organization. Or they don't have the self-awareness to realize how those questions will be perceived. Either way, it is a flag.
- Do they communicate well? Do they think well?
  - The best way to learn how people communicate and think is by hearing them ask questions. Do their questions make sense? Are they logical? Is there clarity of speech? Do they listen and ask good follow-up questions?

The best way to get a quick look inside a person's head is by giving them the opportunity to share their prepared questions and reveal what is in there. The questions you ask them at the end should either be about gaining insight on items from their resume or be organic follow-up questions based on something they asked about that caught your attention or made you curious.

A phone screen provides you with unique data points and a running start on knowing who the candidate truly is. The Reverse Phone Screen does the same, in less time. But keep in mind that the key to phone screens making your process more effective hinges entirely on whether you are able to use it for cutting candidates. Not everyone finds phone screens to be effective mechanisms for narrowing your talent pool. Phone screens tend to be most effective at identifying connection skills, genuine interest, and unearthing obvious flags. But if you try the phone screen (reverse or not) a few times, and are unable to cut candidates, then remove it from your repertoire. There is no point in wasting time on something that doesn't work for you.

WORDS OF CAUTION

I've found that gender and racial bias can have a large influence on phone screens because a primary factor you will use to judge the candidate is their voice. And when it comes to voices, gender is always discernable, and race is often discernable.

Since you can tell a person's gender by their voice, there is no doubt that bias can creep in based on that. Interestingly, I've had conversations with people who adamantly claim they can't tell a person's race by their voice. That may be true in some instances, but not most. It is well-recognized that there are certain cadences, intonations, and pronunciations that characterize ethnic speech patterns. You need to look no further than Hollywood and the voice-over industry for commercials or cartoons to see how certain speech patterns are used to indicate ethnicity.

To overcome this potential bias, you must approach it with the mentality that an accent is simply an accent. Some accents are acquired from growing up in a certain community or growing up with English as a second language. Those accents tell you little more than a British accent, Canadian accent, southern accent, or a Boston accent tell you. The only reason they would signify more is if you make assumptions about the underlying culture or community associated with the accent.

Train yourself to think of ethnicity-based accents as "regional accents." They tell you where the person may have grown up. If a person had an accent that indicated they were from Chicago or New York City, you wouldn't judge them. You'd focus on the content. Treat ethnicity-based accents the same way. You absolutely must acknowledge that this type of bias exists and then move past it deliberately.*

---

* Part 4 contains additional practices that minimize bias and are relevant for phone screens as well.

PRACTICE:

THE RESUME INTERVIEW

The resume is the interviewer's most powerful tool. It is a documentation of every organization the candidate has worked for, their role and title, the length of time they were there, their contributions, their accomplishments, and their education. It even provides the "Other" facts they choose to share to exhibit how complete they are. You could not ask for a better tool to assess someone than their resume. And it has a major flaw—the candidate wrote it.

> You could not ask for a better
> tool to assess someone than
> their resume. And it has a major
> flaw—the candidate wrote it.

The resume is not objective: It is the candidate's version of the truth. This flaw manifests itself in two ways. First, studies consistently indicate that candidates exaggerate on their resumes. A report by ADP Screening and Selection Services discovered that in 2.6 million background checks, 41 percent of candidates lied about their education and 44 percent lied about their work experience.[1] Despite those damning statistics, I rarely find resumes to be full of bold-faced lies. Rather, some accomplishments are inflated, or the candidate has taken undue credit for something they didn't fully own. The bigger concern is that the candidate has applied a filter to their experiences. While some lies of commission may occur, there are certainly some lies of omission.

Many interviewers find resume interviews to be daunting because of the level of detail they are trying to unearth to find the truth. They don't know where to begin nor when they have dug deep enough. Sometimes they don't do them at all. But the same thing that makes the resume flawed is what makes it a powerful interview tool: The candidate wrote it.

Because the candidate wrote it, you can use their own words to drive a fact-based assessment. They don't need to rely on memory. They don't need to hypothesize. You don't need an abundance of questions either. The key is to stay organized and stay tightly focused on four key questions that you will repeat for each role or organization on their resume. Each question focuses on areas central to understanding the candidate.

- Their work
- Fact-checking
- Omissions
- Career Transitions

These are your roadmap and they keep it simple. Your approach during the interview is that of an iron fist in a velvet glove. The velvet is your genuine curiosity to learn more about them. The iron is the ability to apply pressure and challenge them if something doesn't hold up.

START AT THE BOTTOM

Always work through the resume from the bottom to the top. Usually this means from the oldest position to most recent. This approach prevents you from skipping around and potentially losing important details. There are candidates who don't write their resumes in chronological order. Instead their resume is organized by skill type or some other categorization. In those instances, to stay organized, still start at the bottom and work your way up.*

THEIR WORK

Think of each job on the resume as a pit stop where you'll pause, kick the tires, check the fluids, and then move on. If their work history fits on one page, you can discuss each job they've held. If it is two pages or

---

* Trying to put their resume in chronological order yourself, either in advance or during the interview, is a waste of mental and physical energy. I don't recommend the effort.

more, then choose the jobs most relevant to what you need in your role and focus there. If your preference is to work through their entire work history, then plan for more time to be dedicated to the interview.

Either way, you do *not* want to dig into every bullet of every job. Instead for each organization ask:

> **Interviewer:** Tell me the top three skills you leveraged while at LB Hermington & Co. Just list the skills, at this point I don't need examples.

Alternatively, if they've held multiple different roles within an org, you can separate it by role:

> **Interviewer:** Let's start with LB Hermington & Co. As an associate, tell me the top three skills you leveraged, just list them for me . . . . Got it, and as a program consultant what were the top three skills . . . and as the lead manager?

Give them clear instructions to only list their skills: This isn't the interview where you have a lot of time for explanations. You will have time for details and examples in other interviews. At this stage all you are looking for is alignment between the skills they mention and the skills you require. If there is alignment, then you've got an early indication of skill fit.

FACT-CHECKING

In the resume interview your duty is not to confirm everything they say. Purely from a logistical standpoint, this is nearly impossible. Most resumes are full of bullet points, often with statistics or some other measure of success. It would take more than an hour to work through them all in detail. Beyond the logistical difficulty, even if you pressed candidates on details of specific accomplishments, you are still simply asking them if they are telling the truth. No candidate is going to say they aren't telling the truth. Some people who aren't telling the truth will get nervous and potentially provide indication that they aren't being honest. But some people will get nervous even when they are telling the truth. Remember, research shows you won't know the difference.[2]

You do, however, want to get detail on some of their accomplishments. During the resume review, pick three to four that spark your curiosity and ask a few detailed questions. But instead of interrogating them bullet by bullet to determine their trustworthiness, get to the heart of it with one question. For each organization at which they've worked, ask:

> **Interviewer:** When we do reference checks, which of these accomplishments will your managers be able to discuss as evidence of your skill?

The power you have is *not* that you will call their supervisors and work through the resume bullet by bullet. Rather that you *can,* and the candidate knows you have that power.

Their answer should be as close to some version of "all of them" as possible. They could legitimately have reasons why a manager couldn't discuss some of the accomplishments. For example, "My manager was on leave and I pushed the work forward on my own." But if the accomplishment was major, there manager should be aware of it. If, without good reason, they hesitate to state that their manager could verify certain accomplishments, then don't trust what they have written. If this question throws doubt on many of their accomplishments, then don't advance the candidate. If there are one or two that you are now uncertain of, take note of those accomplishments. Are they ones which involve skills you require? In the next interview, focus on those accomplishments to confirm their accuracy and pay close attention to the assessment of the skill areas in question to ensure the candidate has strength in them.

OMISSIONS

Since the resume is the best version of the candidate's career and work experiences, you will need to ask questions that uncover things they omitted. The best way to access omissions is to ask the following question for every organization for which the candidate has worked. If they've only worked in one organization for many years, then ask the same question for several of their major roles.

> **Interviewer:** You had some great accomplishments at LB Hermington & Co. Tell me two or three things you were *not* able to accomplish.

No one accomplishes everything they set out to do. You are looking for someone who can admit their mistakes, is open to learning from them, is self-aware, and remains confident even in defeat. The role you are hiring for will determine what you are looking for in their answer. If they made mistakes that show a lack of skill or awareness in an area relevant to your role, note those for follow-up in ensuing interviews.

Occasionally this set of questions leads to answers that show a pattern of mistakes. For example, the person may consistently under- or overestimate resources, politics, relationships, or skills. That pattern needs to be noted because either they don't learn from mistakes or have no self-awareness. After the interview, you will need to determine if the patterns require you to assess more deeply in following interviews or if you have enough concern about their negative impact that you don't advance the candidate.

TRANSITIONS BETWEEN ORGANIZATIONS

When looking at transitions between organizations, you are looking for patterns that reveal insight on candidates' decisionmaking, priorities, or performance. To identify patterns, ask two questions for each transition between organizations:

> **Interviewer:** Why did you leave this organization? . . . Why did you take the next role?

There are three patterns that should cause you to raise a flag and you will need to consider whether it will impact their ability to thrive in your organization.

"I wasn't looking to leave, but . . ." Some candidates claim they weren't looking to leave, but an opportunity presented itself that drew them away. This does legitimately happen and isn't a flag when it happens once. But if you see a pattern you should be concerned. A person who is committed to their work doesn't constantly have their ear to the ground for the next opportunity. If a candidate says, "I was not looking to leave," more than once, then it indicates the opposite—they are consistently looking for the next opportunity. This potentially indicates a lack of commitment and you should note it as a flag to probe for in other interviews.

"I left because the job turned out not to be what I signed up for . . ." Some candidates have multiple short stints and repeatedly provide the explanation of a job "not being what they expected." This pattern is a sign the candidate habitually builds up their next role to be better than it eventually is. Once they are in the role, the fantasy wears off and they begin to look elsewhere and the cycle repeats.

Some people are genuinely on a journey of self-discovery and consistently take on new things until they find what they want. Job-hopping every two or three years as part of that journey is acceptable. But when the consistent reason for leaving is "not what I signed up for," it shows an inability to take ownership for their decisions. It indicates a lack of understanding that organizations can't build themselves around every individual.

Assuming they advance from the resume interview, find moments in the remainder of the interview process to determine specifically what the candidate needs in their next role. If they have expectations that can't be met in your organization, then cut them from your process. Otherwise, you'll hire them, invest in them, and a year later, they will cut you.

"I was laid off . . ." Given economic turbulence, getting laid off once is understandable, maybe even twice. But two layoffs should get your attention and three or more is a flag.

High performers usually don't get laid off multiple times. But, during economic downturns, even high performers can lose their jobs. During economic downturns, talented people often accept roles lower on the totem pole. Which means they may be first on the chopping block if their new organization struggles as well. This leads to people with every level of talent getting laid off repeatedly. Everyone is then trying to reenter the workforce, and many get turned away because of the stigma of previous layoffs. You may see this on the resumes of candidates who had to fight their way out of those cycles or are still trying.

This is a tough reality, but it is not yours to fix. Empathy should help you build better rapport with candidates and lead to better decisions, but it shouldn't become pity, which can blind you. The rule is straightforward—multiple layoffs are a flag. Stick with that rule. Don't worry about being too harsh, one flag alone doesn't eliminate anyone. Your complete set of interviews and assessments will help you determine if there are enough flags to deny the candidate.

CLOSING THE INTERVIEW

The line of questioning to understand their decisionmaking in job transitions is not because you are looking for someone who will commit their life to your organization. That doesn't happen anymore. When a candidate is strong you will find two things, honesty and a positive pattern of behavior. A positive pattern is logical, indicates a plan for where they are going, and is in alignment with what your organization can provide. You want someone who understands that their best shot at getting to their optimal future is doing the best job they can for the current organization they work for. For that reason, always end the resume review with:

> When a candidate is strong you
> will find two things, honesty and
> a positive pattern of behavior.

Interviewer: How does the role with our organization fit into your career path so far?

Depending on their answer, a good follow-up is:

Interviewer: Every job is a stepping stone to something else. What would this role be a stepping stone to?

For these questions, you are looking for an answer that clearly demonstrates a role with your organization will keep the candidate on pattern. This means they will do great work for you because it will help them get to the next stage of their career. You have to be comfortable with this type of pattern as opposed to being concerned that if you hire them, they will eventually leave. The information you gain can actually be ammunition for what it might take to keep them longer than normal.

INTERVIEW-READY RESUME

The resume interview should be the first interview you do in-person with the candidate. The farther into your process the candidate advances, the higher the odds that you will like them and will want them to do well. You'll be more velvet glove than iron fist. By that point they won't have to lie to you—you'll lie to yourself.

Don't use the resume interview to address every question and curiosity about the candidate or you'll never finish getting through the resume. It is a fact-finding mission and the pacing is fast. Probe only to get more facts. Other interviews will allow you to spend time on the things you noted.

The best way to prepare for this type of interview is to use the four key areas detailed above and take notes directly onto their resume. That allows you to work through the resume from bottom to top. Please see an example of an annotated resume prepared for the resume interview, page XX.

CANDIDATE NAME

EDUCATION

NAME OF GRADUATE SCHOOL
GRADUATE DEGREE

NAME OF UNDERGRADUATE SCHOOL
BACHELOR'S DEGREE

EXPERIENCE

THIRD ORGANIZATION

Managing Director
- Member of the 4-person leadership team that...
- Manage a national program that...
- Oversight of an annual process that attracts 2,000...
- Manage three teams with four direct reports...

Senior Director
- Management of...with additional responsibility for 3 cross-or
- Led the creation of the organization's first strategy for...
- Revamped the internal staff professional development plan...
- Developed a formal career progression/path for 400 employee

Director
- Managed two direct reports, consultants, and all aspects of...
- Implemented the first...More than doubled results from X to X
- Redesigned processes for...
- Created strategic partnerships to further...

SECOND ORGANIZATION

Project Manager
- Directed team of specialists and a staff of 15 part-time employ
- Co-led expansion from 25 sites to 88 sites...
- Pursued new business developments, increased the number of
- Coordinated staff training, site preparation, and program eval

Project Associate
- Evaluated joint venture opportunities...
- Analyzed potential Fortune 500 clients...
- Wrote a comprehensive report detailing...
- Reported directly to Senior Vice President of the division...

FIRST ORGANIZATION

Assistant Manager
- Responsible for programs in 25 regions...
- Hired, trained, and supervised a staff of four to six part-time
- Developed and administered...
- Researched, analyzed, and synthesized information related to...
- Consistently met the needs of over 150 clients on a weekly ba

ADDITIONAL
Conversational Spanish. Avid mountain biker. Familiar with Jav

Annotation boxes:

- How does the role with our organization fit into your career path so far?
- You had some great accomplishments here. Tell me 2 or 3 things you were not able...
- When we do reference checks, which of the accomplishments in this organization...
- Tell me more about your role on this leadership team...
- And how about the top 3 skills you leveraged as Managing Director...
- What are the top 3 skills you leveraged as Senior Director...
- Tell me the top 3 skills you leveraged as Director...
- Why did you leave this organization? Why did you take the next role?
- You had some great accomplishments here. Tell me 2 or 3 things you were not able...
- When we do reference checks, which of the accomplishments in this organization...
- What lead to this expansion? Who worked on that with you?
- How about the top 3 skills you leveraged as Project Manager...
- Tell me the top 3 skills you leveraged as Project Associate...
- Why did you leave this organization? Why did you take the next role?
- You had some great accomplishments here. Tell me 2 or 3 things you were not able to accomplish.
- When we do reference checks, which of these accomplishments will your managers be able to discuss as evidence of your skill?
- Tell me the top 3 skills you leveraged while in this role. Just share the skills, at this point I don't need examples.

The candidate's resume is the best version of themselves. An effective resume interview is important because the best version of a person doesn't always show up once hired. The power of the resume is that it can be used to help determine how big the gap is between the best version and the person who does show up. The candidate who emerges successfully from a tightly focused resume interview is more likely to show up at work as the person they presented themselves to be on paper.

> The candidate who emerges successfully from a tightly focused resume interview is more likely to show up at work as the person they presented themselves to be on paper.

PRACTICE:
THE PROVINCIAL INTERVIEW

Several years ago, my frustration with the limitations of behavioral and situational interviews led me to stumble upon a different interview style. I was in the middle of a behavioral interview with a candidate who had a strong resume and been highly recommended. But he was clearly nervous, and it was impacting his performance. He was having trouble recalling specific examples and when he did draw upon an example, he explained it poorly. To get around the memory issue, I switched to a few situational interview questions. He did better, but our interpersonal connection was suffering, and I was starting to lose faith that I'd be able to accurately assess his skills. Though I trusted the person who recommended this candidate, I wasn't seeing evidence to support advancing the candidate.

In a moment of inspiration (or irritation) I drew on an observation from past interviews. I had anecdotally noticed when I asked a candidate an interview question, the ones who ask me, "Can I talk about something I am working on now?" and proceeded to talk about a current experience tended to do better. I decided to try this on the candidate in front of me and simply said, "What is the next major meeting you are going to have at work?" He looked a bit confused, but replied relatively easily, "At the end

of this week, with one of our analysts and one of our project managers."
I continued, "And what are you meeting about?" The candidate nodded,
a bit more relaxed, "I'm leading a project to figure out how to improve
our performance management. We have years of data on employees,
performance, and previous approaches. We need to pull it together to
come up with a better performance management system."

In that moment the Provincial Interview was born. Since then, I have
continued to use the approach, refined it, and designed a structure to
make it most effective.

The premise of the Provincial Interview is simple. Keep it local and
potentially less rehearsed and polished. Instead of asking candidates
about what they did in the past or what they would do in a hypothetical
situation, ask about something they are currently doing.

THE BASE QUESTION

The key to the Provincial Interview is a base question that grounds the
candidate in the present or near future. It is upon this question that you
will build the remainder of the interview. The base question can take
many forms depending on what you want to assess. Any of the following
can be used as the base question:

- What is the next major meeting you are going to lead?
- What is an upcoming conversation you need to have with
  someone on your team?
- What is an upcoming important request you will need to make
  from someone at work?
- Is there an upcoming performance review that you need to give?
- What is a project you are working on right now?
- What is some research/analysis you are currently conducting?

As with any interview, you must know what you are assessing for.
This will impact the base question and the follow-up questions. As
with behavioral and situational interviews, the Provincial Interview can

be used to assess any skill or quality. It requires a little more flexibility from the interviewer. But if you have the base question and the follow-up questions planned, it is easy to master.

Take another look at the list of base questions above and think about the different areas you can assess with those types of questions. The applicability is wide-ranging: management skills (people, projects, or processes), relationship building, strategic thinking, any functional skills (HR, finance, operations), planning, organizational skills, self-awareness, ability to influence, ability to motivate, communication skills, decision-making, giving feedback, and so on.

FOLLOW-UP
QUESTIONS

Once you've identified the skills or quality you want to assess, pick the base questions that will allow you to assess that area. Then determine the follow-up questions that will allow you to dig in. Each base question with its accompanying follow-up questions is a "set." The Provincial Interview is best when you use multiple sets within one interview. For example, you can ask, *"What is the next major meeting you are going to lead?"* paired with a specific set of follow-up questions. You can spend five to seven minutes on this set. Then ask another, *"What is some research or analysis you are currently conducting?"* with a specific set of follow-up questions.*

The follow-up questions are as important as the base question. The follow-up questions are designed to assess the specific area you need to understand. If you want to assess project management skills, you could pick the following base question and use any of the follow-up questions below it. The row on the right exists only to provide the rationale for the question:

---

* The number of sets you do within an interview is up to you. I generally do two to three sets within one interview, allowing for other questions to also be asked.

Base Question: Think of a project you are currently managing, preferably one that involves or impacts multiple people.	
In 2–3 sentences, what is the goal of the project?	*Provides context for the remainder of the questions.*
What is your role?	*Provides context for the remainder of the questions.*
Who are the main people involved in the project? What are their names?	*Provides context for the remainder of the questions.*
Have you delegated specific responsibilities to specific people? How did you decide what to delegate to whom?	*Delegation of work is critical to project management. If they have the authority to decide who does what, you want to assess how they think through this.*
Give me the name of one of the people on the team. What are they responsible for? Is he/she on track? How do you know if he/she is on track?	*Tracking of work is critical to project management. By picking a specific person, you keep it real rather than hypothetical.*
Do you meet them individually or as a group? How often? When is the next meeting? What is the purpose of that meeting?	*This gives you a sense of their management style. You will learn if they manage loosely or tightly. You will learn if they plan ahead or go-with-the-flow. The judgment is based on what works for your team or organization.*
What is the timeline, e.g., when is the project done? What are the key milestones?	*To manage projects well, you must have strong planning skills, including planning of time and knowing when you are behind.*

When we do reference checks and talk to some of your team members, will they know the milestones?	*Milestones should be known by the project team.*
What do you personally need to get done in the next week? In the next month?	*Self-management is as important as managing others.*
How are you tracking what you personally need to get done?	*Self-management is as important as managing others.*
What are you behind on? Why? Is that a big problem or little problem? Why?	*Everyone is always behind on something. You are looking for an honest answer. They should display a sense of how urgent it is that they catch up. Some things are fine to be behind on. But some things cause a bottleneck for others and can't remain behind. They should be able to identify that.*
What does success look like?	*Do they have a vision?*
What does failure look like?	*Are they realistic about their vision? Are they prepared for hurdles?*

Once you have created the set of follow-up questions, choose which to use and the order that works best as you navigate through their current situation.

The Provincial Interview is versatile. By altering the follow-up questions, you could use the same base question and assess for relationship-building skills instead.

Base Question: Think of a project you are currently managing, preferably one that involves or impacts multiple people.	
In 2–3 sentences, what is the goal of the project?	*Provides context for the remainder of the questions.*
What is your role?	*Provides context for the remainder of the questions.*
Who are the main people involved in the project? What are their names?	*Provides context for the remainder of the questions.*
Outside of this project, how often do you interact with them?	*If they are strong relationship builders, they don't only interact for this specific project. They go to lunch with them or drop by their office to say a few words for a few minutes.*
Who do you know the best? Who do you know the least?	*This sets up the next question.*
Why do you know "NAME OF PERSON" the best?	*Helps the interviewer understand how the candidate gets to know people.*
Why do you know "NAME OF PERSON" the least?	*Helps the interviewer understand how the candidate gets to know people.*
(Interviewer picks a name the candidate mentioned) Tell me something about "NAME" outside of their professional lives. You don't need to share anything sensitive, but if you were describing this person outside of their work life, what defines them?	*Strong relationship building requires a personal connection and an understanding of people outside of just their work skills. Strong relationship builders connect with people as a whole, not just as co-workers.*

(Interviewer picks another name and asks the same question.) Let's do that again. Tell me something about "NAME" outside of their professional lives.	*Strong relationship building requires a personal connection and an understanding of people outside of just their work skills. Strong relationship builders connect with people as a whole, not just as co-workers.*
How often do you meet with this team? Do you meet individually or as a group? Do you meet at the office or over lunch outside the office?	*There isn't a right or wrong answer, external factors might influence this. However, strong relationship builders tend to break out of the normal flow of work to connect with others. They use lunch, coffee, off-site time to build relationships.*
Which of the people is most critical to the success of this project? What motivates him/her? How do you know?	*Strong relationship builders spend time (either naturally or deliberately) getting to know what drives other.*

A base question that I have found very effective is to ask about an upcoming meeting. The example below uses this base question and provides a range of follow-up questions to show the many directions you can go with this style of interview.

Base Question: Do you have an upcoming meeting at work that includes more than one person? (Assuming they say yes)	
What is the purpose of the meeting and what is your role?	*Provides context for the remainder of the questions.*
Tell me the names and roles of the people who will be there	*Provides context for the remainder of the questions.*

How will you influence NAME (a person they mentioned above)?	*If context is relevant this helps the interviewer learn about the candidate's ability to influence.*
Who is most important to the success of this meeting? Who is least important?	*Helps the interviewer understand if the candidate is strategic in how they think about people, politics, and relationships.*
What can go wrong in this meeting? How can you mitigate that?	*Helps the interviewer understand if the candidate thinks ahead several steps. Do they contingency plan? Can they adapt?*
How would a bad meeting look? How can you mitigate that?	*Another way to gain the insight above.*
What will make this a great meeting?	*Helps the interviewer understand if the candidate plans meetings in advance and plans them well. Are they outcome oriented or process oriented?*
How are you planning for this meeting?	*Another way to gain the insight above.*
If you find out you only have half the time you had planned for this meeting, what will you prioritize? Why?	*Helps the interview understand how the candidate thinks, prioritizes, what matters most to them, etc.*

As you continue to use the Provincial Interview, you will build up a library of base and follow-up questions. Once the library is built, you can reuse them time and time again with minor adjustments depending on the candidate.

Provincial Interviews are the best of both worlds, behavioral and situational. They rely less on memory than behavioral questions. They are situational, but firmly rooted in reality because they are based on actions the candidate is currently doing. If you find value in assessing hypothetical scenarios, the Provincial Interview still gives you that flexibility to assess what candidates would do if the situation changed. For example, you can easily ask, *"If your two counterparts on this project quit tomorrow, how will you move forward?"*

The Provincial Interview decreases the pressure on the candidate to create a potentially untrue answer to fit a question or to stretch a prepared example around a question that doesn't quite match it. Someone can still lie about what they are going to do in a meeting, but the questions are less leading and contain less evidence about the desired response.

In addition, this interview style is less likely to favor the quick thinker and therefore isn't biased against the candidate who takes more time to process. Since the questions are based on upcoming events, the processor and the quick thinker are on even ground because both have had time to think about it. In this way, the Provincial Interview favors the strong thinker, the strong executor, and the strong leader, which is what you are ultimately seeking.

> The Provincial Interview favors the strong thinker, the strong executor, and the strong leader, which is what you are ultimately seeking.

PRACTICE:
NEVER INTERVIEW ALONE

As an interviewer, your primary tools are your eyes and your ears. Their job is to gather information. Yet, everything you collect must pass through one more instrument before you make a decision: your brain. Its job is to give meaning to the information. The decisions made about a candidate rely on an interpretation of what the interviewer sees and hears. Even if you do your best to clear the biases, the first impressions, and the inconsistent interviewer behavior—you are still relying on an interpretation. Unless we can claim to be oracles, there is still room for error.

To offset this potential for error, most organizations have the candidate do interviews with multiple team members to gather a range of perspectives. The value in varying perspectives is that they allow you to identify themes as evidence of the necessary skills and qualities you've identified. If, upon discussion post-interview, all the interviewers report similar strengths and agree on a few qualities, then those are likely true. If they disagreed on some criteria, that is also helpful because it tells you what to focus on for the next round of interviews.

The logic behind this common best practice is clear. No individual person can see a candidate from all the angles necessary to make a good judgment. Few organizations, however, make the connection that multiple perspectives are not only valuable *across* interviews, but also *within* interviews. An interview is a single moment in time. It is very risky to have that moment interpreted by a single person.

As such, the practice to adopt is to always have candidates interview with two interviewers at the same time. Multiple perspectives within the same interview are critical to understanding the candidate for two reasons. First, we often hear what we want to hear rather than what was meant. Second, sometimes we don't hear at all or don't remember what we heard.

ONE RESPONSE EQUALS
TWO ANSWERS

Studies have shown that two people can hear the same exact response and interpret it in very different ways.[3] Your perspective is the lens through which everything anyone else says is filtered. Sometimes you will hear what your own experiences will allow you to hear. In those cases, if your perspective is not aligned with what's needed for the role, you may make bad decisions. I've seen the following happen on many occasions:

> Sometimes you will hear what your
> own experiences will allow you to hear.

Co-interviewer 1: I really didn't like the way he described tutoring underprivileged kids.

Co-interviewer 2: I thought it was admirable.

Co-interviewer 1: Come on, he went to Ivy Leagues for undergrad and grad school. It was so condescending, it came off like "I help the poor people who aren't as good as me."

Co-interviewer 2: I got the sense that he worked hard to get into those schools. I'm not sure, but my guess is he comes from humble roots, not privilege and now he's trying to make sure other kids have the same shot.

Co-interviewer 1: Did you hear what he said about the kids' neighborhoods? He said "those" kids grow up believing that welfare is a normal part of life. Who is he to judge?

Co-interviewer 2: I kind of agreed with him, I didn't think he was judging, I just thought he was stating a fact.

Co-interviewer 1: Are you serious! I don't even know you. You're lucky I didn't interview you when you applied to work here.

Who's right in the discussion above? I don't know. But the point is that if only one of these two interviewers had interviewed the candidate then that discussion never would have happened. Either the candidate would have been assessed as condescending and arrogant or as selfless and empathetic. Having two people's viewpoints allows for a conversation about gray areas that one person would have seen as black or white. It allows you to use the subsequent interviews to uncover more or to share the discussion with others who also interacted with the candidate.

Focus and Memory

There are times when you are interviewing someone, and you momentarily lose focus. The candidate is talking, and you begin thinking about something else. Their voice becomes a drone. We all have lives outside the interview room pulling our minds away from what is occurring in that moment. The scientific name for this phenomenon is stimulus-independent thought, and it is defined as "streams of thoughts and images unrelated to immediate sensory input."[4]

Sometimes one of those thoughts takes hold during an interview and you've suddenly missed half the candidate's response to a question. This happens much more often than we realize. A study that collected data from over 15,000 participants in eighty countries found that, on average, our minds wander 47 percent of the time.[5] The data indicated that our minds wander the least during sex (10 percent) and the most during grooming activities (65 percent). I'm certain the act of interviewing isn't even remotely comparable to the low end, but the focus needed to interview likely brings it below the average. Let's assume our minds wander 20 percent of the time during an interview. For an activity of its importance, we are still missing out on a considerable chunk of information. This doesn't include other times, post-interview, when we simply forget what the candidate's response was or the nuance of what they said. Having two people interviewing simultaneously reduces those odds.

> **Co-interviewer 1:** I don't recall the candidate mentioning anything about getting input from the rest of her team. That's a problem if we want a person who collaborates.

> **Co-interviewer 2:** Actually, she did. Remember when she mentioned the project she led in Boston and she pulled the full team together to brainstorm ideas.

Co-interviewer 1: You are right, I missed that in my notes. Not sure what happened, I must have blanked.

Having two people interview the candidate at once cuts down on any issues caused by lack of memory or loss of concentration.

The Logistics of 2:1 Interviews

It may seem logistically difficult and time-consuming to have two people interview a candidate at every stage. It can be difficult, but you should think of it as a worthwhile investment. If you can't do it for every stage, prioritize it for the final interviews. Those final interviews count the most and there is less room for error. If someone slips through an earlier interview you will catch them at the final interview. If a single interviewer is unsure about a candidate's skills, qualities, or motives in an early round, they should note it for follow-up in a two-person interview at the final round.

The final round shouldn't just be one set of two-person interviews. The final round should have at least two sets of interviews. In each interview, two interviewers should assess the candidate together. With that structure, the accuracy of the assessment is raised dramatically. From a time and logistics perspective, this is a far better use of four people's time than if each of them interviewed the candidate individually.

Avoid this 2:1 Mistake

When using co-interviewers, avoid creating an uneven power dynamic such that one interviewer will simply agree with what the other decides. For example, don't put your boss and a newly hired person together. The new hire will agree with whatever your boss says.

The Boss: I hated that candidate.

New Hire: Agreed. I could *not* stand him. Repulsive!

The Boss: People like that don't deserve to work anywhere.

New Hire: I know a guy who can put a hit on him. He'll never work anywhere, ever.

If possible, the power dynamic should be relatively even. That isn't always possible, so at a minimum, always set the right tone and expectations up front with your interviewers. Tell them that it is okay to disagree with each other. They need to know that they don't have to arrive at the same decision. Finding common ground to agree upon defeats the purpose of having multiple perspectives. If they had different opinions but came around to the same opinion before you had a chance to discuss the difference with them, you would lose something important that could be further assessed. Keeping the multiple perspectives is critical to sound assessments.

If co-interviewers agree with each other, that's great. That validates their assessment more. If they don't, that's also great. Discuss who heard what, why they believe what they believe, and whether it aligns with what the other interviewers assessed in their interview. Make it clear that during the post-interview discussion you want to know if they have different opinions because that is where the truth exists.

Each interview is one of only a few occasions to get a snapshot of the candidate. That snapshot needs to be clear and from as many angles as possible. Never leave it in one interviewer's hands or you'll end up with a less-than-accurate picture of the candidate.

BREAK DOWN
THE FOURTH WALL

*I*n the world of theater, the fourth wall is the term for the imaginary wall between the audience and what occurs on the stage. This wall exists in the world of interviewing as well. In an interview, you are the audience and the candidate is on the stage. Since you can't step onto their stage, you must observe from your seat and determine if the story being told is an accurate reflection of reality.

Ideally, the best way to assess a candidate would be to follow them around in their current job for an extended period, the way anthropologists do. Dr. Daniel Miller, noted anthropologist from University College London, has summed up perfectly the issue with interviewing as well as his approach to resolving it.[1]

> Mostly what people say is the legitimation of what they do, not the explanation or the description . . . . It is better to be immersed in people's everyday life and also listen in to the conversations they have with the people they live with, rather than carrying out the artificial procedure that we call an interview. In my more ethnographic works I look more to people's interactions with things, and the evidence for what they actually do.

In the hiring process, following a candidate around at their current job is impossible. Yet, as Dr. Miller suggests, you can still learn how the candidate interacts with things, gather evidence of what they do, and have your own conversations with the people they interact with.

Work sampling, in-basket assignments, and reference checks are three powerful ways to gain that insight. The traditional interview as your only mechanism means you must rely on learning about the candidate through their recounting of events. Using these additional approaches breaks the fourth wall and gives you a completely different lens to look through.

PRACTICE:
WORK SAMPLING

Anyone who has every hired a website designer knows that process requires the potential designer to show previous websites they've built. If you were to hire an architect to build a house, you'd ask to see previous plans, blueprints, and photographs of that person's work. Work sampling is the same idea and means having the candidate bring recent work product(s) to the interview for discussion. Interviewers tend to be very comfortable using this approach when they are hiring someone for a creative role or any other job that results in a physical product. Why don't interviewers do this to assess every job for which they are hiring?

One answer is that people don't do it because it isn't the norm. It's different and therefore uncomfortable. Concerns with confidentiality also tend to make interviewers hesitate. Asking a candidate to share something they are working on feels like an intrusion into the professional space of the other company. You don't want to put the candidate in the awkward position of feeling like they are being asked to share something they shouldn't. It also just seems like more work.

None of these hurdles are insurmountable. That fourth wall needs to be torn down. You have to shake things up to learn the most you can about your potential new hire. If you don't break the norm, don't complain when you end up with the norm.

> If you don't break the norm,
> don't complain when you
> end up with the norm.

Since work sampling isn't the norm, candidates may not know what to expect when you ask for it. Be transparent from the moment the candidate enters the interview process. They should know they will be asked to submit a work sample, preferably during the second round of interviews or later. You don't want to review work samples as part of the first interview because you don't know yet which of their skills you can use the work sample to further explore. To explain the process, whether in writing or verbally, use the following:

> During the second round of interviews, you will be asked to submit a work sample. This should be something you've previously created at work that shows your ability to do that job well. This is one of the best ways for you to demonstrate your skills. You will not be asked to provide anything that is confidential or that you are not allowed to share. After the first round we will further discuss what your options are.

A clear sense of the skills you are hiring for will determine the type of work sample you need to request. Website design and architecture aren't the only jobs that have a work product; nearly every job has some physical byproduct of the work. If you are hiring for very technical skills, those are the easiest work samples to gather. But even more general skills can be assessed. If you want a sense of their analytical skills, have the candidate submit spreadsheets they built or any other analysis they have conducted. If you are looking for communication skills, request reports or memos they've written, or PowerPoints they've presented.

If you can think of a relevant work product, then you shouldn't hesitate to ask for it. The sample doesn't have to match perfectly with the skill you are assessing because the questions you ask will be the key to successfully gaining the insight you want. The discussion with the candidate should feel similar to the way you talk to a current team member who is working on a project. This "fourth wall" approach has the added benefit of giving you a more realistic feel for the candidate outside of interview mode.

The questions are always driven by what you want to know. For example, if a candidate submitted an analysis in Excel and you want to understand their analytical rigor, then the questions are focused as follows:

- What made you decide to pull this set of data?
- What were you trying to discover?
- What other analyses could you have run?
- What did you have to do to manipulate this data and get it in a usable form?
- Walk me through some of the more complex portions of this analysis.
- What decisions were you able to make from this analysis? What decisions were you not able to make?

On the other hand, if you wanted to learn more about how they present data or communicate it, then include a different set of questions:

- How would you explain this to someone who doesn't understand data?
- Are there multiple audiences for this data? How did you present it differently?
- What is the story you were trying to tell with this data?
- Was there something you didn't want the audience to ask? What if they did ask that question?

Regardless of what you are assessing for, there are a set of questions you must always ask at the end of the work sample interview if they haven't been answered yet:

- How much of this did you create yourself?
  - (*If relevant*) Who else was involved?

- How long did this take you?
- Who was the audience?
- What part of this did you enjoy? What part did you not enjoy?
- What result came out of this?

The work sample you want candidates to bring is something that was primarily created by them. If others worked on it with them, it allows you to ask about how they collaborated and worked together. Their answer to how long it took lets you know if they work quickly enough for the pace of your role or organization. Knowing their audience helps you understand why they framed it the way they did, but also the importance of it. If it was for their boss or senior leadership then it should be high quality. If it was for themselves, then lower quality is acceptable. Knowing your definition of quality lets you use their audience as a gauge. Understanding what the candidate enjoyed and didn't enjoy tells you whether they will like similar work if you hire them. Learning what came out of this work gives you further context on its importance, quality, and effectiveness.

Confidentiality can be a hurdle when requesting work samples. There are some work products that people can't share, and you must respect that. Interestingly, I have never had a situation where confidentiality concerns resulted in getting nothing from the candidate. In those situations, we discussed and mutually settled upon what they would share. Here are some solutions to get around that issue:

- Often, whatever they are sharing can be "cleaned." In other words, they take out anything that connects it to real people or organizations. They replace actual names with "Name" and actual organizations with "Organization X," "Organization Y," etc.
- You should never ask to keep the candidate's work documents. Explain up front that they will bring the work samples in. You will discuss them together and they will then take the sample when they leave. Nothing gets left behind.
- Explain on the front end that a limited number of people on your team will view the work samples and anything the candidate shares will be kept confidential.

There are some industries where this approach might not work. Corporate espionage is real. If you are in an industry or organization where this could be an issue, then don't use this approach. Seeing their work product isn't about stealing the trade secrets of a competitor or getting insight on a competitor. If that is your intent, you are going down the wrong path. Work sampling is about tearing down the fourth wall and seeing firsthand the quality of a candidate's work as well as the quality of their thought process.

PRACTICE:
IN-BASKET ASSIGNMENTS

The interview is a proxy for how well the candidate will do on the job. But the rubber doesn't hit the road until they start working and you see their abilities firsthand. There is no reason to wait to see what they can do until the first day of the job. Do it as part of your interview process. An alternative to work sampling is to have the candidate do some of your work.

> There is no reason to wait to see what they can do until the first day of the job. Do it as part of your interview process.

In-Basket Assignments are activities you give the candidate to complete in advance and then you discuss them during one of the interviews. Think of In-Basket Assignments as homework for the candidate. The approach takes some up-front preparation by the interviewer but can be used time over time and do not have to be complex or require a lot of planning. The key is to choose assignments that mimic the work they will do on the job. They will vary depending on the role. Here are a few suggestions to give a feel for what you can create.

Have them create a presentation: If public speaking or any form of presenting is part of the job, have them do it as part of the interview process. Give the candidate instructions explaining that this skill will be part of their job. Instruct them to create a presentation (PowerPoint, Prezi, etc.) in advance and submit it. Provide them with thirty minutes to present to a small group, followed by Q&A. This allows you to assess their communication skills on several levels. You can assess their strength in creating presentations, their ability to deliver the presentation, and their ability to answer questions on the spot during the Q&A. For the Q&A, assemble a group of five to seven employees to serve as the audience. Share with them the context and instruct them to think of questions to ask for the Q&A. Give them a very basic rubric (scale of 1 to 5) and ask them to score the candidates on the qualities that matter most to you (presence, oral communication, professionalism, presentation content, etc.)

Have them do analysis: If any form of analytical work will be required, provide an In-Basket that tests their analytical skills. If they need to expertise with Excel, provide them with a set of data and instruct them to manipulate the data or identify facts based on the level of expertise you require (V-Lookup, Pivot Tables, etc.). Once the analysis is submitted, check it for accuracy. During the interview ask more questions using the analysis as the basis:

- What conclusions can you draw from this data?
- Are there trends that stand out to you?
- How long did this take you to complete?

Have them review part of your strategic plan: If you have a strategic plan, copy a portion of it, no more than three pages, into a separate document. Make sure it is a portion that is self-contained, and the candidate won't need more than what you share to understand what is on the page. The assignment is for them to read the portion of the strategic plan and come prepared with as many questions about it as they want. They should also be prepared to answer questions about what they read. For example:

- Do you think the money we've allocated for this is too high or low?
- What are the downsides of pursuing this approach?
- If you had to prioritize the four tactics in the plan, how would you prioritize?
- If you had to cut one of the ideas, which one would you cut and why?

Have them research a topic and write a memo: Ask the candidate to research a topic that is relevant to your organization and provide a recommendation. If your organization uses memos, then have them write a memo. If not, then they can simply write the assignment in another format. As an example:

- Research everything you can about Salesforce, our CRM software. Write a two-page memo recommending whether we should use it for tracking candidates who apply to our organization.

Regardless of the assignment, conduct the discussion with the candidate the same way you would with a team member. Try to recreate what it would feel like to have a meeting with you. That will give you a better sense of what working with them may be like. It also has the benefit of giving the candidates a feel for the work and what interaction as a team member is like. The interview is a glimpse of each other and In-Basket Assignments are a perfect opportunity to make it a two-way experience.

PRACTICE:
REFERENCE CHECKS

There is a saying in real estate that serves as advice to buyers, *"Don't fall in love with a house until after you close."* This advice is to prevent buyers from consciously or subconsciously overlooking anything that could be wrong with a house they really like. Once they own the house and move in, the things they convinced themselves were minor suddenly become major.

This same advice applies to candidates and interviewing. "Don't fall in love until after you close" is analogous to "Don't fall in love until after the reference check." In practice this can be difficult because, chronologically, references are done after the interviews are complete and you believe you've found the person you want to hire. Reference checks often don't feel like part of the interview process because they aren't done for every single candidate, just the finalists.

But it is a mistake to view reference checks as something that occurs after the interview process is done. The purpose of the interview process is to gather information, and reference checks gather really important information. A reference check has the potential to turn your star candidate into someone you have to deny, the same way a bad interview could. You must be ready for that. The correct mentality is that reference checks are an integral part of the interview process. This mental reframing is small but important because it keeps you from falling in love before the close.

A reference check has the potential
to turn your star candidate into
someone you have to deny, the
same way a bad interview could.
You must be ready for that.

Too often, reference checks become a "check the box" activity. Instead of being used to continue to assess the candidate, they are mechanical and done in a way that confirms what you want to hear. This happens primarily because by this point in the process you *want* to hire the person. I have made the mistake of not acting on critical feedback a reference once gave me about a candidate. I was already mentally invested in the candidate and wanted them to join the team. So, I rationalized what the reference told me. Within three months, the reference check was ringing in my ears as this person struggled on my team. The issues I had told myself would not be a problem—even though clearly articulated by the reference check—were definitely a problem. I'll never make that mistake again.

Reframe how you think about reference checks. Think of the reference check as the final interview. You are still interviewing the candidate, but through the eyes of the people who worked with or managed the candidate—people on the other side of the fourth wall.

Who Should Do the Reference Check?

You have two choices. Have someone who wasn't connected to the interview process do the reference checks or have one of the interviewers, potentially even their potential manager, do the call. The benefit of having someone outside your process do the call is that they will be more objective. They are not personally invested in the candidate and therefore more likely to hear and report back the truth. Ultimately, this lack of personal investment is also the downside because it can impact the connection with the reference.

A personal connection to the decision helps with overcoming the perception that the reference check is a separate and tactical step that gets shipped off to someone in another department. It keeps the reference check within the interview process. More important, an interviewer can ask the questions in first person with more authenticity because they have spent time with the candidate. To demonstrate this point, consider the following:

> A person who is *not* on the interview team is assigned to do a reference check for a candidate who they have no connection

with. Let's call the candidate Ronald Sims. When this person
calls the reference check they will likely ask a question along
these lines, *"Can you give me examples of Mr. Sim's strengths?
. . . And his development areas?"*

Compare that to the following:

The person who does the reference check has also interviewed the candidate. She calls the reference check to gather
the same insight. But their conversation begins with, *"I've
had a chance to spend some time with Ron (she can call him Ron
because she met him and knows that is what people call him) and
have identified some of his strengths. Can you give me examples
of Ron's strengths? . . . Ron mentioned that he is working on
improving his public speaking skills, what is your assessment of
that? . . . From your experience, if there was another thing that
we could help him develop, what would that be?"*

In this case the interviewer exhibits familiarity with the candidate,
which serves as a form of common ground and builds initial trust with
the reference check. Personalizing the experience increases the odds of
having a better conversation and therefore gathering more information.
The more the reference will open up to you, the better.

If the manager has the capacity and discipline to be objective, I recommend having them do reference calls. The benefits of learning more
truth are worth the effort. Delegating reference checks may save you
time in the short run, but if they contribute to a wrong decision, you'll
lose more than you gained.

Tone of the Call

You want the tone and framing of your reference check to be inquisitive,
advice-seeking, and supportive of the candidate. You don't want the
person providing the reference to be defensive, you want to keep them

open. You don't want them too worried about what they divulge; you want them to trust you. You set this tone with the preamble before you start the reference check. Always include the following line:

> **Interviewer:** We are interested in learning more about Ron, his strengths, accomplishments, but also areas of development that we can potentially help him grow in. You've worked with him and know all those sides of him, so I appreciate you sharing your insight, so we have a greater understanding of the talent in our process.

This isn't just a tactic to build trust, this should genuinely be the purpose of the call. The truth is, you don't want the reference to say bad things, but you do want the truth. The majority of the time the truth does help you understand, onboard, and support the candidate. You don't need to explicitly mention to the reference that sometimes the truth can cause you to deny a candidate. That is implicitly understood and doesn't need to be brought up because it will close more doors than it will open.

TWO QUESTIONS TO
ALWAYS ASK REFERENCES

A great question for uncovering helpful information is, *"In six months there is always a moment where I find myself saying, 'I wish I had known X about this person.' What will 'X' be for this candidate?"* This is a great question because it is true, everyone has had this experience, and it is not necessarily a bad thing. This type of authentic question changes the mindset of the person providing the mindset. They know this will happen and want to help. The information you gain from this question is rarely information that causes the candidate to not be hired, rather it is insight that helps you manage them better if you do.

In addition, always ask the following question at the end of a reference check, *"Would you hire this person again?"* Their answer must be an unequivocal yes. If you detect hesitation, caveats, or anything resembling "maybe," proceed with caution. Keep in mind, the reference is the person the candidate deemed best for you to talk to. And the reference knows they should be saying glowing things. If they would hesitate to rehire your candidate, then you need to consider if you should hire them at all.

WHEN A CANDIDATE IS HESITANT TO PROVIDE A REFERENCE

There are times when a candidate is honest about a negative relationship with a current or recent supervisor. As a result, they indicate that they don't want you to speak to that person. There are a few options for moving forward:

- You can ask them for recent performance reviews to assess their work.
- You can talk to several other people at the organization in question and triangulate their feedback to determine if your candidate's reasoning is valid.
- You can insist that you speak with the reference anyway and tell the candidate that you will take the candidate's perception and honesty into consideration.

The third option is the best because you usually end up regretting not having heard from their current or recent supervisor. Even if the reference is someone whose motives you question, you still have the ability to stack their thoughts against what other references said and what your interview process has told you. You'll have done a lot of work by this point to assess the candidate, make sure the final step is done just as thoroughly.

GENERAL TIPS FOR REFERENCE CHECKS

There are several other tips for the reference check process that maximize what you'll learn:

- Always inform your reference check that you will keep the information confidential (which you should). This increases the odds of hearing the truth.
- Take good notes during the call and save them for a year.
- Do at least three reference checks, two of which should be supervisors. At least one supervisor should be current, the other should be within the last three years. Supervisors will give more honest assessments and tend to have a more accurate view on performance. If this seems too much to you, then at least one must be a supervisor and the other two should be people who worked closely with the candidate.
- Make sure your candidate gives you permission to contact their reference checks in writing. Email is fine, but it needs to be documented.

HEARTBREAK HAPPENS

Reference checks provide information that help you understand the candidate. Usually, that turns out well for the candidate. But when it doesn't, it is a painful experience. You have to be prepared for the day when a reference check causes a candidate to be denied. This never feels good and is worse than denying a candidate earlier in the process because everybody loses. You are heartbroken because you thought this candidate was the one. The candidate is heartbroken because they thought they were the one (why else would you be doing reference checks? No one gets denied based on references they provided . . .). And the people who provided the reference are often confused, feel guilty, and may follow up with you to determine if it was something they specifically said. The fear of feeling this way is part of why reference checks aren't done as rigorously as they should be. When people fall in love, they don't want to be heartbroken.

The best way to get comfortable knowing that a reference check may eliminate your favorite candidate is to be open about it with your candidate. This is the mirror image of the reference check preamble described earlier in which the potential for denial is implicit. With the candidate you must be explicit. Before the reference check process begins, let the candidate know the following:

- No offer will be extended until the reference checks are complete and satisfactory.
- Your reference check process is thorough, and it can cause an offer not to be made. Explain that this will not be based purely on the reference checks, but on the big picture, and that the reference check is just another assessment serving as a data point.
- Put all of this in writing so there is no question or confusion that can lead to legal issues.

MANAGING HEARTBREAK

If you do deny a candidate because of reference checks, do *not* tell the candidate which references provided the information that led to the decision. If the candidate asks, tell them your HR policies will not allow you to do that. If you don't have that as an HR policy, create one.

Explain that even at the reference check stage, there were specific areas in which you needed more information, and the references are the final stage of gathering that information. Assure them that none of their reference checks purposely tried to torpedo them. (I've never had a reference check intentionally doom someone. If a reference did intentionally give a bad reference, then skip this assurance.) You can share the concern, but you *cannot* share who validated the concern, even if the candidate asks. That respect is what you owe to the reference checks for their help. That confidentiality is critical. You must protect those relationships.

These are tough calls to make. Your framing has to be one of transparency about why you made the decision. It should be clear you are sharing an insight the candidate needs to be aware of and that the decision is in the best interest of all. The blend of resolve and compassion you exhibit in those moments matters tremendously. The candidate will not like the decision in the moment but will respect you in the long run.

• PART 4 •

IDENTITY
AND BIAS

When a candidate sits at the interview table with you, they represent two people: the person they are, and the person you think they are. The bigger the gap between reality and perception, the higher the odds of the wrong decision being made. The opening chapters discussed the interference that fills that space. There is another culprit whose existence serves to keep reality and perception apart. That culprit is bias.

I've had the benefit of interviewing side-by-side with talented professionals from a range of backgrounds. The strongest of these professionals not only know the impact of societal beliefs, they know the fallibility of their own decisionmaking processes—and they prepare for it. This section is focused on making effective hiring decisions at the intersection of identity and bias.

BIASES ARE
UNSPOKEN CRITERIA

*D*uring the 2016 Vice-Presidential debate, Mike Pence took umbrage with Hillary Clinton for suggesting unconscious bias could be a reason for officer-involved shootings. Their opposing beliefs generated countless spirited discussions in the national media about bias, with arguments falling mostly along political lines. But for organizations focused on finding great talent, the debate about unconscious bias was an old one, not at all politicized and already settled. All scientific evidence supports the conclusion that bias exists. Next steps were clear as well: Dedicate resources to managing its impact on talent.

Silicon Valley, which had increasingly been under pressure for its lack of diversity, had become the public face for addressing bias in the workplace. In 2013, Google began conducting employee trainings on the impact of bias on hiring, retention, and performance. More than 75 percent of their 70,000 employees have gone through the training and they've since made the content publicly available.[1] In 2015, Facebook also publicly shared an internal training course on the impact of bias on hiring.[2] Many others have taken on similar work, including those outside of tech. In 2018, it was Starbucks's turn. After two African-American men were arrested at a Starbucks in Philadelphia while simply waiting inside for a friend, the company closed 8,000 stores for an afternoon to conduct bias training for 175,000 employees. The materials for that training have also been made available for anyone to use.[3]

In organizations that are tackling diversity with earnest, the question about bias has shifted from whether it exists to discovering the best way to minimize it. Based on the painfully slow pace of change, particularly in Silicon Valley, it's tempting to believe training isn't a particularly effective method. It doesn't help that several studies—one done at Harvard that included thirty years of data and another one a meta-analysis of 429 other studies—indicate that diversity trainings, in general, haven't historically been effective.[4]

These studies don't imply that diversity can't be dramatically improved. There is quite a bit of good news in the research. Not surprisingly, they found that the quality of the training and how it is framed impacts its effectiveness. They recommend additional mechanisms such as gaining buy-in from managers by engaging them in solving the concerns and increasing their contact with underrepresented employees. Also effective are targeted strategies such as mentoring, college recruitment, and task forces for improving diversity.

It's worth noting that none of the research suggests organizations shouldn't tackle bias at the interview stage. Rather the research shows that addressing issues of identity in the workplace requires dedicated effort and a multi-pronged strategy. A critical part of that strategy is interview practices. Interviewers are the gatekeepers: If you can't bring diverse talent into your organization, you won't have anyone to benefit from the retention and performance strategies proven to be effective.*

In my current role, I have been fortunate to work for an organization where these types of studies don't simply sit on a shelf. We consistently translate them into actual effective practices, and we are proud of the results we've achieved. Our senior leadership team is 50 percent women.

---

* I recommend learning from the studies mentioned as well as the resources provided by Facebook, Google, and Starbucks. Improving diversity will take more than interview practices. It involves shifting company culture, analyzing employe retention, gaining buy-in, having courageous conversations, and a range of other approaches.

Several years ago, our staff and leadership shifted toward majority people of color. Our board of directors has had a similar transformation and now is 40 percent women and 50 percent people of color. We've come a long way from an environment that initially wasn't diverse by any measure.

That evolution began like most diversity efforts. We formed an internal diversity task force and we took a hard look at ourselves. We created a diversity statement and began to collect data on everything from our demographics to hiring trends to our culture. The task force eventually evolved into a "diversity council" with rotating membership from across teams. Over time we continued to layer in strategies; advocacy by senior leaders, "diversity champions" who advised hiring managers, affinity groups, anti-bias workshops, leadership stories in which team-members shared their life experiences, book clubs focused on authors representing a range of identities, and interview practices that supported diverse hiring.

The participants in the external leadership development programs we operate are also very diverse across multiple measures. These outcomes don't happen by accident. They are the product of specific organizational practices whose impact we monitor through qualitative and quantitative data. One of the areas in which our organization has been collecting longitudinal data is the impact of our interview practices. Statistical analysis of our data shows that the commitment to interview practices described in this chapter has led to a 75 percent decrease in the effect of bias on our hiring decisions.

Similar to the approach with first impressions, it would be naïve to believe we can completely eliminate all bias. Some research even suggests, though with mixed results, that the more we try to suppress a thought, the more likely it is to rebound later.[5] That isn't how our brains work, so elimination isn't the goal. The goal is to recognize bias, control it, and minimize its ability to negatively affect outcomes.

DEMYSTIFYING BIAS

Unconscious bias isn't one particular function of the brain, it is the result of a wide range of cognitive biases.[6] But in practice, biases fall into two categories: the ones people will admit to, and those they won't. The biases in that second category tend to include race, gender, sexual orientation, religion, etc. Unconscious or not, the larger problem is those beliefs are rarely discussed. Yet the biases that spring from them lurk in our minds during the interview, quietly impacting our decisions. They become unspoken criteria that wedge between who the candidate is and who we think they are. While those biases must be overcome, most people and organizational cultures aren't ready yet for that level of discourse and vulnerability. And in some cases, if the message about bias is delivered as a compulsory change, people become *more* entrenched in their beliefs.[7]

Your goal isn't to suddenly shift everyone's unspoken beliefs through a set of interview practices. Your goal is to make them aware of how their beliefs can negatively impact their behavior and how increased self-awareness makes them better decisionmakers. You won't get far if you start with a discussion about their most controversial biases.* Instead, leverage the research that shows an effective approach to managing bias is to tap into people's desire to be fair-minded.[8]

> Your goal is to make them aware
> of how their beliefs can negatively
> impact their behavior and how
> increased self-awareness makes
> them better decisionmakers.

To get there, start simple by explaining that bias isn't a dirty word defined exclusively by racism, sexism, homophobia, or the like. Rather bias has its roots in the cognitive strategy of categorizing the world around us. When you talk about tackling bias, start with the dictionary definition:

> a preference for one thing over another, especially an unfair one; a partiality that prevents objective consideration of an issue or situation

---

*   Biases based on identity (race, gender, etc.) are discussed in the next chapter.

A bias is just a tendency to believe some categories of things (people, ideas, products, etc.) are better or worse than others. Synonyms for bias include "non-objectivity," "partiality," and "one-sidedness."

Whether a bias is helpful or hurtful depends on whether the underlying belief is relevant or not. It is important for people to understand the concept before layering in the societal beliefs that can make it harder for people to accept their own role in perpetuating those same beliefs. Gaining this understanding helps us approach our own potential biases in a more informed and open way.

For example, I've never liked ties with cute things on them. If it has hammers, palm trees, or dolphins on it, I start to question a candidate's professionalism. My belief is that a tie isn't the place to show personality in an interview. I believe the candidate's choice of tie tells me something about their decisionmaking. I'm not quite sure what it tells me, but it isn't positive.

This bias comes from my experiences in business school. My background is rooted in the working class. People around me didn't go to college. I was one of the few who did. I went to UCLA and it felt like a foreign country with its own rules and customs. I gradually found my way, adjusted, and graduated. Going to graduate school was the next step. If college was a foreign country, business school at Stanford was on another planet. Not just with its own rules and customs, but language and dress code as well.

When I got to Stanford, I didn't own a suit. I soon learned organizations looking to hire were always on campus hosting events. So, I bought a suit. Dark gray. I also bought ties—boring ones with no personality. I made the decision to be conservative in my appearance. I wanted to convey one clear message: "I'm a smart serious professional."

Later, as a recruiter, that focus on appearance and perception was still there, impacting my thinking as I judged candidates. A bias against cute ties might be relevant if I am hiring a spokesperson for a conservative clothing line. But more often, a tie tells me nothing about whether someone can do the job for which I'm hiring. My belief about ties says more about me than about any candidate. It is an irrelevant bias that will cloud my judgment, affect my decisionmaking, and be a barrier to assessing talent.

These types of seemingly innocent biases, such as preferences for strong handshakes, types of attire, or certain personality traits are where you want to start. They get people to acknowledge that bias exists. The focus on better decisionmaking is the first step to effectively taking biases out of the shadows and decreasing their impact on the hiring process.

The focus on better decisionmaking
is the first step to effectively
taking biases out of the shadows
and decreasing their impact
on the hiring process.

PRACTICE:
THE BIAS LIST

In many ways, the practices in this book emulate methods found in cognitive behavioral therapy (CBT). CBT is a combination of behavioral and cognitive psychology with a focus on improving mental health. It was originally designed to address depression but is now used to improve mental health in other areas as well. CBT focuses on changing cognitive distortions (beliefs, biases, and thoughts that happen automatically) and their associated behaviors through specific coping strategies.

Dr. David D. Burns, professor emeritus at the Stanford University School of Medicine, is the foremost expert on CBT. His bestseller, *Feeling Good*, is filled with templates and worksheets designed to help his clients take control of their automatic thoughts and change their behavior. According to Dr. Burns, to change your behavior you must, "Train yourself to recognize and write down thoughts as they go through your mind."[9]

In the same fashion, the first step toward controlling biases is to think about what your biases might be and write them down. To increase the odds of accurately assessing someone else you must recognize the triggers of certain emotions, assumptions, and reactions in you. Putting thoughts in writing is a powerful way to make your thinking concrete. This mechanism for capturing the "unspoken criteria" makes it easier to manage. It allows you to compare your biases against the actual criteria needed for the job. Below is a list of some of my biases:

- I don't like candidates who give weak handshakes.
- If a candidate has a heavy accent, I worry it will affect their impact at work.
- I do like candidates who lean forward when I'm talking.
- I like when candidates ask me questions about my own experiences.

As evidenced by my list, biases can turn you against someone or pull you toward them. You need to be aware of both because they are equally dangerous. A bias *for* someone will cause you to give them the benefit of the doubt and you'll hire someone because you feel comfortable with them, regardless of their strength as a candidate. A bias *against* someone will cause you to not only withhold the benefit of the doubt but to discount their talent.

As with first impressions, the point is not to immediately view biases as wrong but to stop them from hijacking your decisions before you have a chance to determine if they should be part of your criteria. For example, a common bias I encounter among interviewers is against candidates who don't make strong eye contact. If I'm hiring for a position which requires the person to quickly build trust with people, then that bias is relevant. If I'm hiring a data analyst, it is less relevant. The lack of eye contact may be awkward and makes it harder to interview them. But I need to assess their ability to look at data, not look at me. That's the trust I need and the skill I need to focus on. Documenting that I have that bias in advance allows me to control it rather than having it unconsciously control me and cause me to miss talent.

As with first impressions, the point
is not to immediately view biases
as wrong but to stop them from
hijacking your decisions before you
have a chance to determine if they
should be part of your criteria.

When you initially begin the practice of documenting your biases, you may only be able to list a few. Keep documenting. Self-awareness takes time and you generally only notice your own quirks when they occur in the moment. A way to effectively and gradually identify these is to start actively paying attention to your judgments upon first meeting people—anyone, not just candidates—and then logging them.

That list of biases you generate, long or short, will keep you honest. If a candidate exhibits something from your list, being conscious of it steels you against it unduly affecting your decision. It gives you the ability to step back and objectively assess your subjectivity. With this practice I now catch and control thoughts like, "Okay, ring on his thumb. I'm not a fan of those, but it probably doesn't matter. Let's see what he knows. Let's see what he can do."

Eventually that mental practice will become a habit and you'll be surprised how quickly your mind could have gone down a path without you being aware of it. Your bias list is a flashing yellow signal. Not stopping you, just causing you to slow down. A reminder that you haven't reached your decision yet and need to keep focusing on the road still ahead.

Using this practice to capture the unspoken criteria when you are the only one listening is a step in the right direction. Now let's raise the stakes a bit.

PRACTICE:
SHARE YOUR LIST

The downside of a bias list is that it requires you to hold yourself accountable. Research indicates we are more likely to believe others are biased and have a much harder time believing we are biased.[10] In other words, we are biased against believing we are biased. Because of that dynamic, it is helps to have others hold us accountable.

Once you've started the practice of creating a bias list for your personal use, consider supercharging the practice by sharing the bias list with a co-interviewer. The success of this practice rests on the interviewing team trusting each other enough to share their biases without fear of judgment. This trust may come from time spent together or from a leader on the team role-modeling the vulnerability needed to acknowledge your own biases.

Most of the biases people will openly share won't be the deepest, most controversial ones. Your team may not be ready yet to discuss the complexities of race, gender, or sexual orientation. Some people don't want to let go of their biases: They believe they are accurate and may even be proud of them. That is regrettable but can't be ignored. What you want as a first step is the basic understanding and acknowledgement that our minds make decisions quickly based on inputs that we aren't aware of.[11] The more complicated discussions can get layered in over time as trust grows, comfort with vulnerability increases, and the practices are bought into.

If you are doing this with a group of interviewers, have them discuss their bias list with each other the day before interviewing anyone. During the interview, nothing explicit is done with the bias list other than each interviewer having their own heightened awareness. It is after the interview, when interviewers are debriefing the candidate, that they must hold each other accountable. They must be willing to share their biases and call each other out if needed. This may not happen often, but setting that expectation of accountability means that a post-interview discussion may go as follows:

> **Interviewer 1:** I didn't really like the candidate, I thought his answers to most of the strategic thinking questions were average at best.

> **Interviewer 2:** I thought he did well on the strategy questions I asked. I know you've mentioned that you don't like when candidates use their hands a lot. I just want to call that out because he sure did use his hands a lot.

Interviewer 1: Yeah, I noticed it, but that wasn't the problem. His answer to the second question, for example . . .

Or the discussion might go as follows:

Interviewer 1: I didn't really like the candidate, I thought her answers to most of the strategic thinking questions were average at best.

Interviewer 2: I thought she did well on the strategy questions I asked. I know you've mentioned that you don't like when candidates use their hands a lot. I just want to call that out because she sure did use her hands a lot.

Interviewer 1: She did! I couldn't get past it, I'm staring at her hands the whole time . . .

Interviewer 2: But what about the content of answer? If you get past her hands, what did you think about her answer to the second question, the one that focused on strategy . . . ?

A team of strong interviewers comfortable with each other can have the second type of conversation and keep each other honest. If you aren't fortunate enough to have a group of interviewers with those types of established relationships, then let's consider another practice that allows you to leverage bias lists.

PRACTICE:
CLEAR YOUR BIAS

Since a team of interviewers is often pulled together from various parts of the organization, it may not be feasible to share bias lists. But taking biases out of our subconscious and revealing them is still important. An alternative to sharing bias lists is to instruct interviewers to create their bias list for personal use, and then implement a post-interview debrief protocol. Begin the debrief with a description of the protocol:

> **Lead Interviewer:** Team, one of our protocols is that for each candidate, the first thing we do is lay out on the table anything about the candidate that may have biased you for or against him. We'll do a quick go-around, get those biases out if they exist and then let's focus on what we were really looking for. Our first candidate was Jerry. Any biases we need to get out? Was there anything outside of the answers he gave that caused you to favor him or not favor him?

> **Interviewer 1:** Don't judge me, I just don't like it when a person gives me the two-handed handshake. I know they think they are being sincere, but I automatically think it's fake.

> **Interviewer 2:** Funny, I reacted to the same thing, but I actually like it. It makes them seem genuine, I liked him from the start.

> **Lead Interviewer:** Did anyone else have concerns about authenticity? No? Okay, it seems that wasn't necessarily a concern for others, but it could be important for this role. I'll jot down "authenticity," so we've captured it. Anything else . . . ? No? Then, let's do everything we can to put those initial impressions aside. Let's get him back to neutral and let's focus on what we came here to determine. Let's discuss his response to question one . . .

This protocol allows several things to occur. First, and most important, it allows the unspoken criteria to be spoken. The potential biases are no longer sitting in heads without scrutiny. Second, by jotting the biases down, it validates the perspectives of the people who shared their biases. Admitting a potential bias isn't easy. Acknowledging that an interviewer may have picked up on something increases the odds they will be open to sharing again in the future.

Acknowledging the bias doesn't mean it is accurate, it means the person has beliefs.* It creates an environment in which people will begin to speak more openly. Once biases are openly aired, the team can discuss whether others had the same reaction and whether the issue matters for the role in question. That doesn't mean you'll automatically change your decisions. It just means that you've taken the time to determine if the inputs to the decision are relevant and whether they reflect reality or perception.

ADDITIONAL
BENEFIT

The approach of demystifying bias and leading with general biases versus more controversial biases, has an interesting additional benefit. Across many years of using this approach I've learned that a reduction in any biases (innocent or otherwise) tends to have a larger benefit for candidates from underrepresented groups. This is partially because many of people's innocent biases overlap with the biases that make underrepresented groups "different" in the first place. In addition, the act of raising one's self-awareness doesn't limit itself to the innocent biases, it also raises one's awareness of societal biases.

---

* It is likely the word "bias" will meet resistance by some people. It has become a buzzword almost solely associated with diversity efforts. Know your audience. If this is the case, replace "bias" with "assumptions" or "automatic thinking." If you've used any of Kahneman's research, use "system 1 thinking." The goal is to get people to understand how their minds work. If the term you use creates resistance, use a different one.

> Across many years of using this approach I've learned that a reduction in any biases (innocent or otherwise) tends to have a larger benefit for candidates from underrepresented groups.

By reducing biases of any kind, we tap into our desire to be fair-minded and good people. People may not acknowledge their societal biases, but practices such as these make it harder to deny them and those benefits extend to candidates who are historically the most impacted.

BE MINDFUL

*B*iases based on race, gender, or other elements of identity have deeper history and are more engrained in our psyche than any others. They are the biases whose existence is most likely to be denied because no one wants to believe they are racist, sexist, or any other similar label. If someone knows they have these beliefs, they usually know better than to openly display them in the workplace. They are the ultimate unspoken criteria. They rarely show up in a discussion on first impressions, nor will you likely find them directly addressed on a bias list.

The practices shared so far are steps forward. But depending on the culture and leadership of your organization, they may represent the upper limit of what you can introduce into your interview processes. That is an unfortunate reality you may have to face. That does not mean you've reached the limits of how far you can push yourself.

The strongest interviewers I've worked with all understand that missed talent occurs when they let their minds run on autopilot. Gaining control of first impressions and creating bias lists helps disrupt automatic thinking. But the best interviewers take it a step further. They spend time specifically learning about issues related to identity. They also spend time thinking about what they think about those issues.

"Thinking about what they think" is a subtle nuance worth exploring. One level of learning is to gain exposure to issues of identity that others may struggle with. A higher level is to then question what you believe about those issues and why you believe them. That practice of introspection is a type of mental preparation called mindfulness.

Psychologist Dr. Jill Suttie defines mindfulness as a mental state that involves an increased awareness of our emotions, thoughts, and surroundings, accompanied by a sense of nonjudgment. Research has shown that mindfulness can be used to overcome the impact of bias and prejudice on decisionmaking.[1]

The healthcare industry has been on the forefront of this approach because the decisions that doctors and nurses make are influenced by societal beliefs and have life or death repercussions. For more than a decade there has been a growing body of research indicating the harmful effect of unconscious bias by clinicians on health outcomes for patients.[2] To counter this effect, researchers recommend clinicians engage in mindfulness practices to "reduce the likelihood that implicit biases will be activated in the mind, increasing providers' awareness of and ability to control responses to implicit biases once activated."[3]

Depending on your background, your reaction to using mindfulness practices may be to think of them as too metaphysical to be practical. While some studies do recommend clinicians use meditation to foster mindfulness, they also recommend practices that use selected readings, web-based tools, and guided discussion.[4] It is the latter practices that you should leverage as effective mental preparation for combatting bias.

PRACTICE:
MINDFULNESS THROUGH READING

As our previous practices show, to disrupt bias, you need to increase awareness of it in general and more importantly increase awareness of when it is activated. To disrupt biases specific to identity, you need to specifically think about those types of biases—you have to be mindful of them. Increasing your mindfulness can be achieved by reading an article about the impact of implicit bias on issues of diversity shortly before you interview. After you read it, reflect on what you agree with and what elements of the reading might apply to your thought processes.

A simple internet search will provide a wealth of reading options.* The reading does not need to be long nor does it need to be complex. If you have capacity, do this practice the evening before you interview and then peruse the reading again the day of the interview, shortly before you conduct it. Brief moments of this specific type of mindfulness have been shown to create positive effects against bias. The purpose is to make you think about what you may be thinking. It is to remind you to be fair-minded and to make better decisions.

If your team is at a point where they are also open to this practice, assign an article as a required pre-reading for all interviewers. The group practice is identical to the individual practice—read it the night before, reflect, and peruse again shortly before the interview.

An additional step to disrupt the bias even more is to gather your interviewers before any interviews and discuss the reading with them. The purpose is not for anyone to publicly admit their identity biases. Rather, the practice is an opportunity for people to share their thoughts on the reading. A set of guiding questions helps set the tone:

- What parts of the reading did you agree with? Why do you think you agreed?
- Was there anything you didn't agree with? Why do you think you disagreed?
- How would you describe the concept of bias to others?
- Do you think it can get in the way of effective decisionmaking? Why or why not?
- Have you had any personal or professional experience with this previously?

---

* One that I recommend beginning with is entitled, "Outsmarting Our Brains: Overcoming Hidden Biases to Harness Diversity's True Potential."

As the leader of this meeting, your role is to model the correct mindset by sharing your own thoughts, acknowledging that biases exist and explaining that they negatively impact decisionmaking. Explain this intent transparently. The purpose is for the interviewers to be more mindful of their biases. If they spend a short amount of time thinking about what they may be thinking during an interview, they've increased the odds of controlling the effects of those thoughts.

PRACTICE:
MINDFULNESS THROUGH THE IMPLICIT ASSOCIATION TEST

If you are open to pushing yourself even farther, a similar activity can be done using the Implicit Association Test (IAT). The IAT can be found online and is an activity designed by researchers at Harvard University to inform the test-taker of their biases in a range of areas—race, religion, weight, age, and more can be assessed. The test is based on how quickly you associate positive or negative prompts with the specific topic of potential bias. The speed with which you associate the prompts indicates an underlying bias.

The research behind the approach is based on neuroscience, but also has detractors who claim its results are unreliable.[5] Given that, it is important to keep in mind that using the IAT for mindfulness is *not* about correctly identifying your biases. What matters is that by taking the test, you are thinking more deeply about how your mind works. You are using it to *question* your assumptions, how you make decisions, and how you see the world around you.

For this practice to be effective, go to the IAT website and choose which test you want to take (they are categorized by different categories of identity). After you take the IAT, it will provide you with results indicating whether you potentially have a bias and to what degree. The next step is to ask yourself, *"If this outcome is true, why would that be?"* Assume for a moment the outcome is accurate and reflect on why you may believe what you believe.

- What experiences could have informed that viewpoint?
- Are they relevant?
- Are they what a fair-minded person would think?

Finally ask yourself, *"How can I make sure this bias doesn't unfairly impact my decisionmaking during the interview?"*

Like the mindfulness attained through reading, this practice can be adapted for your interviewers. Again, the practice is identical and can be done at the individual level. Should you choose to take it a step farther, you can have a pre-interview group discussion based on the experience of taking the IAT. The discussion with your interviewers should not be about everyone revealing their IAT results. Rather the topic of discussion should be their reaction to the IAT.

- What was it like taking the IAT?
- Were you concerned about the results you might receive?
- How would you describe the experience of taking the IAT to others?
- Assuming the test is accurate, how can these types of biases get in the way of effective decisionmaking?
- Have you had any personal or professional experience with this previously?

If you or anyone else in the room has the courage to share their results from an IAT test, that can be done as well. But be cautious because it can be counterproductive unless there is strong trust among the interviewers. That decision depends entirely on the culture of your organization and its maturity on this topic. If these types of discussions are very new to the organization, I do not recommend revealing personal biases (either in the IAT discussion or the article discussion). Very likely, the trust within the group hasn't been built up enough to go that deep. That is

---

* The IAT may also indicate that you do not have a bias for the category you selected. If it indicates you don't have a bias, then ask yourself, "How can I make sure I maintain this neutrality during the interview?"

fine; the mindfulness created by the activity matters and the leadership you exhibit by opening the door to the conversation carries weight that will improve decisionmaking.

The topics of implicit bias and identity are complex ones. Successfully addressing them depends on your organization's current practices, beliefs, and culture. It also depends on your organization's readiness to address the issues. For that reason, attempting to capture all the nuances of deeply entrenched societal biases in one chapter, or even two or three, would be a disservice. An entire book can be written on the topic, and many have been. Two books I recommend are *Whistling Vivaldi* by Claude M. Steele and *Blind Spot* by Mahzarin Bahnaji and Anthony Greenwald. Read them both and begin the process of understanding and conquering the many biases within us all.[6]

CULTURE FITNESS, NOT CULTURE FIT

"*C*ulture eats strategy for breakfast."

Peter Drucker, the leadership guru once described as "the man who invented management," is credited with this insight on how to lead organizations.[1] Though some question whether he actually said the phrase, it was attributed to him posthumously by Mark Fields, CEO of Ford Motor Company, and has been cemented into business lore ever since. Drucker isn't alone in heralding the importance of organizational culture. Influential business thinkers like Edgard Schein and John P. Kotter have written extensively about building strong organizational cultures.

With good reason. An abundance of studies indicate that organizational culture positively correlates to organizational performance. Regardless of the culture of the individuals themselves, feeling connected to their organization makes a tremendous difference. Whether in Taiwan, Serbia, or the U.S., research has shown when an employee fits an organization's culture, their commitment and tenure increases.[2] "Culture fit" is particularly important when an organization is going through change, which in today's competitive landscape is an argument most leaders should pay heed to.[3]

It may have seemed odd to include a chapter on organizational culture in the Identity and Bias section. But an organization's culture is its identity. That identity is "an internalized cognitive structure of what the organization stands for and where it intends to go . . . a sense of identity serves as a rudder for navigating difficult waters."[4] The fit between the organization's identity and the candidate's identity is as important as the relationship between any two people. Given this, the idea of interviewing for culture fit seems like a worthy investment.

In recent years, the practice of assessing candidates for culture fit has come under scrutiny because it can have a negative impact on diversity and inclusion. Determining a candidate's fit with your culture can harbor bias based on the candidate's identity, sometimes in coded language, sometimes in plain sight. The pushback against culture fit isn't just a byproduct of a more progressive generation of workers. Some of the same research highlighting the benefits of strong organizational culture also provides evidence of how that culture can harm women and people of color.[5]

> ## Determining a candidate's fit with your culture can harbor bias based on the candidate's identity, sometimes in coded language, sometimes in plain sight.

This tension reminds me of a quote by Nobel Prize–winning physicist Niels Bohr, "The opposite of a fact is a falsehood, but the opposite of one profound truth may very well be another profound truth." Organizational culture is a key ingredient to organizational performance. And culture fit can harm candidates and employees from underrepresented groups. Both are true.

While we can't solve the issues of improving organizational culture in the pages of this book, we can solve the issues associated with interviewing for culture fit. Whether a candidate fits the organizational culture is too important to not assess because their talent won't be applied in a vacuum. The quality of talent is contextual, and organizational culture is that context. Recognizing that the environment in which we work either hinders or supports us allows you find people who are supported by your culture, as well as support those who your culture may be hindering.*

When it comes to interviewing, most organizations either haven't defined their culture with enough specificity, or they haven't translated it into a clear set of assessments. Poorly defined culture cannot be used as a valid hiring criterion. To effectively assess culture fit, you must first define your organizational identity and build relevant criteria around it. This will reduce the vagueness and subjectivity that tends to be the entry point for irrelevant bias.

PRACTICE:
DEFINE AND THEN ASSESS CULTURE

In industrial and organizational psychology, the technical term for culture fit is "person-environment fit" and is defined as the compatibility between an individual and a work environment that occurs when their characteristics are well matched. The problem is that person-environment is often conflated with one or more other categories of fit: person-job, person-group, or person-supervisor.[6] Cornell University's Center for Advanced Human Resource Studies (CAHRS) did a study on recruiter perceptions of applicant fit. This excerpt from their research puts the issue in plain language:

> Examination of interview transcripts suggested that despite the recent emphasis on unique organizational values, strategies, or cultures in discussions of fit, by far the most frequently mentioned determinants of fit were either (1) job-related coursework or experience, or (2) generally (rather

---

*   The process of creating effective assessments may also provide insight on ways to improve your culture. A good question to ask yourself after this practice is whether your culture differentiates you from other organizations but is universal enough to not present a barrier to diversity.

than uniquely) desirable personal characteristics such as articulateness, positive personal appearance, and good general communication skills.[7]

This excerpt allows two problems to come to light. One, when people believe they are assessing culture fit—they aren't. A person assessed in the way describe above could be determined to fit culturally, but then flounder because of the culture. Or vice versa, the assessment could be the person doesn't fit the culture, when that was never assessed in the first place. Second, this ambiguity is where bias creeps in. It allows the term "culture fit" to be used to eliminate candidates based on "articulateness, positive personal appearance, and good general communication skills" and a host of other characteristics often associated with identity. This may be unintentional because interviewers aren't clear on what they are assessing, so they default to their preferences. Or it could be intentional because fitting into the culture requires candidates to look, talk, and behave like everyone else.

Either way, to gain clarity you must separate culture fit into its four categories. When you are discussing a candidate's fit during a post-interview debrief, use the categories as a framework for discussion. This will help determine what you are truly assessing for, and whether it is relevant.

Person-Job Fit

Is the person a fit for the job? This is what you should already be assessing through any questions related to the candidate's skill or knowledge. If another form of "fit" comes up during a conversation about the candidate's skills, refocus the discussion on, "Can they do the job they'll be hired to do? And how well?" Remind your interviewers that "culture fit" matters and it will be discussed, but better decisions will be made if you take it step by step.

Person-Supervisor Fit

Will the person work well with the manager? This is also less directly related to culture fit, but it is important to assess. The manager and the team interviewing the candidate must know what it takes to work well with the manager and should ask the following questions to directly assess it:

- Think of a supervisor you worked particularly well with. What made that relationship work?
- Think of a supervisor you struggled to work well with. What caused that relationship to be more difficult?

This assessment is straightforward. You are listening for items in the answer that indicate if they will do well with their potential new manager. If concerns arise here, then you can isolate them as ones related to working with the manager, not the culture. There are instances where the manager's concerns also overlap with culture fit. In other words, the manager represents and embodies the aspects of the culture that this candidate would struggle with. This is still an important distinction to become aware of because it gets to the specifics of why a decision is being made. Knowing if you are potentially missing talent because of a manager, the culture, or both is valuable and would otherwise stay hidden inside "culture fit."

Person-Environment Fit and Person-Group Fit

The two remaining areas are now "person-environment" and "person-group." Defining these two allows for an effective assessment of what "culture fit" should capture. They will determine what factors of your culture matter and could be hurdles for a person new to the team. If your organization has "core values" or a "mission statement" embedded into the culture, then that is a great place to start. Begin by building questions that assess if the candidate shares those values, beliefs, and norms.

In some organizations, however, "core values" and "mission statements" don't do much more than hang on the wall. In those cases, take a moment to reflect on how things get done by the organization and by the people, and the norms built around those actions. Before you begin asking the candidate questions, you need to first ask yourself several questions to understand your identity as an organization.

What Is Our Organization's Approach to Work?

Determine how your organization (as an entity) operates using questions like the following:

- Is our organization entrepreneurial or traditional?
- Are budgets reviewed weekly or quarterly?
- Are decisions made top-down or does hierarchy play less of a role?
- Does data drive actions? If not, what does?
- Is technology heavily leveraged? Is it used to make things move faster, save money, improve communication, or for some other reason?
- Are new hires extensively trained or expected to hit the ground running?
- How is performance rewarded?

Once you have identified how your organization operates as an entity, prioritize areas and build direct questions around those that matter the most:

- Have you worked primarily in entrepreneurial environments or traditional? Any preference?
- How tightly do you prefer budgets to be managed? Does it make you nervous if no one has mentioned the budget the entire month?
- Which of your previous organizations leveraged technology the most? What did you like about it? What did you not like about it?

How Do the People In Our Organization Approach Work?

This is about how the people interact and work together. A way to think of this is "office culture." If someone steps outside the bounds of "office culture," it isn't a problem because of an official protocol, but rather because colleagues raise their eyebrows and shake their heads.

- Does punctuality matter?
- Do people regularly leave for lunch or eat at their desks?
- Do people listen to music while working or not?
- Do people collaborate a lot or work primarily in silos?
- Is there an unwritten dress code?
- Do people hoard supplies or share them easily?
- Do people primarily communicate via email or live conversations?

Again, prioritize and create questions that focus on what matters the most:

- In your most recent role, what was the preferred method of communication? How did that work for you?
- Do you prefer to collaborate or work alone?
- How much did punctuality matter in your previous organization? What was your opinion on it?

Often, for questions like those listed above, the candidate may want to hedge. When given a question with two options, they may try to give an answer that doesn't hurt them either way:

Candidate: I've worked in both entrepreneurial and traditional environments and really enjoyed them both. I'm really flexible.

Or . . .

Candidate: There are times when I want to collaborate and sometimes working alone is just as great. Some of my best work has come from time spent alone and then collaborating on what I came up with . . . or vice versa . . .

In any of these situations, either get ahead of it by using the Equal Choices structure from Strategy 3 or be prepared to push them: *"If you had to choose one, which would you choose? Don't worry about right or wrong, just tell me which way you lean."*

Having distinct conversations on person-job, person-supervisor, person-group and person-environment allow you to much more clearly identify the inputs to your decision. If your interviewers' reactions are subjective, that will be easy to see. But that is why the practices focused on organizational culture are in the Identity and Bias section. You will need to leverage the previous strategies and practices, including those from Reducing Interference, to determine when subjectivity is helpful and when it is noise.

PRACTICE:
IN THE ZONE . . . OUT OF THE ZONE

As much as possible, questions to assess culture fit should be customized to your specific culture. But once you've defined your organizational culture you can experiment with another approach. The following series of questions allows you to naturally assess the candidate's ability to fit into your organization, but you will need to be prepared to probe, redirect, and push.

- Pick a time in your career where you felt you were "in the zone." By that, I mean you were producing great work and enjoying it at the same time.
- What were some of the results you accomplished during that time?
- What where the key things that allowed you to be "in the zone" and get those great results?

Here is an example of how this plays out with a candidate:

Interviewer: Pick a time in your career where you felt you were "in the zone." By that, I mean you were producing great work and enjoying it at the same time.

Candidate: A few years ago, when I worked at General Motors, I had a role as a . . . . etc.

Interviewer: What were some of the results you accomplished during that time?

Candidate: I built a fantastic team, we were able to develop more partnerships than . . . etc.

Interviewer: What where the key things that allowed you to be "in the zone" and get those great results?

Candidate: Well, we had a flexible work schedule which was great because a lot of our partners were in other countries. We built had a culture that was really collaborative, also . . . etc.

This short series of questions provides insight in several areas. The first question is rooted in their past and doesn't require them to think about your environment. The second question allows you to gain a sense of what the candidate considers to be high performance. It is then up to you to determine if that is the level that you also consider high performance. The last question tells you the conditions or environment that brought out the best in them. Take note of those factors and determine if your organization or role will provide similar conditions.

You will follow up on those factors in a moment. But first get a sense of when they were "out of the zone" by asking a similar series of questions:

- Now pick a time in your career where you felt you were "out of the zone." We are now talking about the opposite of what you just described. Your performance wasn't great and you were not enjoying the work.
- And if you distilled down that "out of the zone" experience, what were the key things that threw you off, made it tougher to perform well?

Here is an example of how this plays out with a candidate:

> **Interviewer:** Now pick a time in your career where you felt you were "out of the zone." We are now talking about the opposite of what you just described. Your performance wasn't great and you were not enjoying the work.
>
> **Candidate:** I would have to go farther back for that, when I first started at General Motors, I initially took on a role as . . . etc.
>
> **Interviewer:** And if you distilled down that "out of the zone" experience, what were the key things that threw you off, made it tougher to perform well?
>
> **Candidate:** one of the first things that comes to mind is the relationship between manager and the team, the manager wasn't strong, because of this . . . etc.

In the above series, you may notice I didn't ask about results. That is because if their definition of poor results aligns with mine, great. And if their examples of poor results aren't bad by my standards, then the candidate has a higher bar than me and I'm fine with that. That context is less helpful, so skip it and save time. For "Out of the Zone" questions, you want to get straight to identifying the conditions.

As they are talking, make sure to list the conditions that put them "in the zone" or "out of the zone." As an example, let's suppose for the "In the Zone" question, they mentioned the following:

- Really structured environment
- Ability to bounce ideas off multiple team members

And let's suppose for the "Out of the Zone" question, they mentioned the following:

- Lack of organizational processes and systems
- Being micromanaged

Let's assume you need someone who can work in an unstructured environment. The first thing to notice is that the need for a structured environment is demonstrated in *both* the "In the Zone" and "Out of the Zone" questions. There is no need to ask more questions on that topic at this point because it is clear the candidate needs more structure than less.

Instead, now is the time to probe with a few behavioral questions around the other intersections. To do this, look for things the candidate mentioned during the "In the Zone" experience that *don't* exist in your organization or team and things they mentioned in the "Out of the Zone" experience that *do* exist in your organization or team. Let's suppose in this particular role, the person will primarily be working independently. That means you would want to start a line of questioning as follows:

> **Interviewer:** You mentioned having people to bounce ideas off of helped you stay in the zone. Have you had a role or project where you didn't have others to bounce ideas off of?

(You then use follow-up questions to learn more.)

Let's say hypothetically they will be working with a new manager. Since they mentioned "micromanager" as an answer in "Out of the Zone," then your line of questions begins with:

> **Interviewer:** When you've previously taken on new roles, what are steps you've taken to get to learn how your manager operates?

(You then use follow-up questions to learn more.)

After you've asked a few of these questions, each having evolved from what they shared, you can determine if you need to further assess their fit in these specific areas. If they haven't done well answering questions about other skills they will need, then there is no need to investigate further. You now know this person won't do well in multiple areas required for the role.

"In the zone" and "Out of the zone" questions lead to more relevant answers about what culture or environment is a fit for them. In addition, there is far less telegraphing. The candidate may still wonder what the "right" answer is, but since your question evolved out of *their* answer it has a more natural flow and therefore is more likely that what you learn is closer to the truth. The downside is because you are relying on them to define "zone," you will receive answers that also include person-job and person-supervisor. The value of having the four categories as a framework still remains because you can parse out what is relevant or not.

CULTURE FITNESS

This chapter is entitled *Culture Fitness, Not Culture Fit* for two reasons. The first is to serve as a reminder that before you assess for culture fit, you need to get your culture in shape. On one hand, you may be in an organization where that means you need to improve your culture. That's unfortunate, but as you work to solve that problem, you will still be hiring people into that culture. On the other hand, you may have a good culture, in which case you need to get the *definition* of your culture in shape. Either way, for the sake of accurately assessing people who can operate within your culture, you must tightly define your culture so you can make strong decisions.

The second reason for using the word "fitness" brings us back to the topic of bias. While your organizational culture may not be constantly changing, it should be constantly strengthening. A culture that is constantly strengthening requires openness to pressure from new perspectives and approaches. Fitness signifies the opposite of status quo and stagnation. If you're culture is "fit," bringing in people who force you to stretch is healthy and an opportunity to consider rather than avoid. To achieve culture fitness, there are two practices to help you redefine whether a candidate is a "culture fit."

PRACTICE:
CULTURE ADAPTABILITY

Whether you intend to or not, when you determine that a candidate is not a culture fit, you are implying something else as well—that the candidate can't adapt to your culture. If the thing preventing you from feeling confident about hiring them is culture fit then ask yourself, "Can this candidate adapt to our culture?" This question opens the door to possibilities that may otherwise be missed. Before eliminating the candidate, ask questions to assess adaptability.

- Have you been in a situation, personal or professional, that required you to adapt to your environment?
  - How long did it take to adapt?
  - Did you ever feel fully comfortable? How did that impact you?
  - What advice would you give someone else facing a similar situation?
- Have you switched between organizations or teams that were different from one another?
  - Was one of them a more natural fit for you? Why?
  - Were you able to adjust to the other one? Why or why not?
  - Did you learn anything about yourself from those experiences?

You are looking for evidence that the candidate is self-aware and knows what works for them. You want that coupled with indicators they are open to change, recognize that not all environments will meet their needs, and have a level of confidence or enthusiasm for entering spaces where they aren't initially comfortable.

Strong candidates know they won't always step into an environment tailor-made for them. Don't assume that is what they need. Take this extra step to increase the odds of finding talent that others often miss due to false assumptions.

PRACTICE:
CULTURE ADD

Assessing for adaptability overcomes an assumption about the candidate's ability to adjust but brings with it a separate assumption that needs to be considered. Assessing for adaptability assumes the candidate is the one who needs to adapt and that your culture won't benefit from the very things that make this candidate different. Once again, before coming to a verdict involving culture fit, spend a moment in self-reflection. Ask yourself, "Can this candidate add something to our culture that we may not realize we need?" Perhaps this candidate not "fitting" could be valuable in terms of their personal experience, thinking style, identity, or other indicator that may initially signal a lack of compatibility.

> Assessing for adaptability assumes the candidate is the one who needs to adapt and that your culture won't benefit from the very things that make this candidate different.

When it comes to identity, your organization's and the candidate's, you need as much help as possible. So, get the candidate's input as well with the following question:

- Based on your experiences either with us so far or your experiences in other organizations, what insights, viewpoints, or perspectives can you bring that others might benefit from?

When identifying what makes a candidate not a fit for your culture, be specific. Then look at those factors and view them as potential assets rather than deficits. Take into consideration what they view as assets as well. The mental exercise isn't intended to overturn every decision. Organizational culture exists for a reason, and part of that reason is to create an environment where people can do their best work. But even in high-performing organizations, not everyone is immediately a high performer.

The relationship between person and environment—culture fit—is powerful because it is a special relationship. It drives performance. It increases commitment. It holds organizations together as they navigate change. The practices in this chapter highlight another benefit of that relationship. By taking the time to make sure either your culture or your definition of culture is fit, you heighten the probability that the talent you hire can reach their full potential. Organizational culture viewed through that lens helps find great people, but also helps build great people. Those people in turn will strengthen and build a great organization.

• PART 5 •

CLEAR
TARGET

The competencies a candidate needs to be successful will adjust depending on the role. Although there is no single set of competencies for all roles, there are four competencies consistently named as critical to success. These four are also consistently more difficult to assess than others: *strategic thinking, continuous improvement, creativity, and emotional intelligence.*

Regardless of the role, some subset of these are always needed to do the job well. And as you seek talent to fill leadership roles, you will find that these all become increasingly important to assess accurately.

STRATEGIC THINKING

*F*or more than thirty years the Management Research Group (MRG) has been a global provider of assessment-based human resource development systems. Their focus is the creation and application of assessment tools that combine business and science to help individuals and organizations excel and grow. MRG regularly conducts studies to gain insight on organizational practices. One such study, conducted across twenty-six industries and more than 140 countries, evaluated 60,000 managers for their leadership effectiveness.[1] The managers were evaluated on twenty-two leadership competencies, included areas such as communication, results-orientation, innovation, and persuasion. Effectiveness in these competencies was measured across twenty separate characteristics such as credibility, people skills, business aptitude, and future potential.

The study found strategic thinking was up to ten times more important to effectiveness than any other competency and nearly fifty times more important than any tactical behavior. A follow-up study with 10,000 executives found that when asked to identify behaviors most critical to the success of their organization, strategic thinking was chosen 97 percent of the time.

With those types of results, it's no surprise that most organizations assess for strategic thinking. What is surprising is that most organizations that assess strategic thinking are assessing the wrong thing. They are actually assessing critical thinking.

Strategic thinking is not the same as critical thinking. Critical thinking is a component of strategic thinking, which is where the confusion occurs. Critical thinking is the ability to solve discrete problems. When you assess for critical thinking you are determining if a candidate can identify an issue, get to the root cause, and find a solution. Strategic thinking is being able to identify an issue, get to the root cause, and then recognize that there might be multiple root causes and several paths forward.

Strong strategic thinkers are able to discern that "if X happens, it could lead to A, B, or C. Which means we'll have to do 1, 2, or 3." Strategic thinking is the ability to connect the dots, anticipate roadblocks, and plan for contingencies. Critical thinking is needed at any one of those decision points. Putting it all together is strategic thinking. It is the ability to see the forest *and* the trees. Critical thinking requires intelligence. Strategic thinking requires intelligence and creativity, judgment, decisiveness, and planning—often in the midst of ambiguity.

There are many traditional questions you can ask that are designed to assess strategic thinking:

- Give me an example of when you participated in developing a business strategy. What was your role? How did you approach it?
- Is it more important to be a detail-oriented person or a big-picture person? Why?
- Give an example of a time when you identified a need for a new approach or product to meet a market need.
- How do the duties and responsibilities of your recent position relate to the organization's strategy?
- Tell me about a time when you had to engage in future planning.

These questions highlight the difficulty in assessing strategy. Individually, they don't tell you much about the candidate's strategic thinking.

They can tell you if the candidate understands what strategy is, but not if the candidate thinks strategically. They can tell you if the candidate has done strategic work, but you won't know how well. You would have to ask the full list of questions to assess strategic thinking. For each one you would also have to dig in with multiple follow-up questions. Even then, you may get answers drawn from multiple examples and not get a cohesive sense of their ability to think strategically.

Strategy is *how* a person thinks. *How* they approached the problem. *How* they solved the problem. *How* they decided on next steps. To assess a competency as abstract as *how they think*, it would help if you could climb into the candidate's brain and witness their thought process. Since that is impossible, what you'll use instead is a set of practices for turning the abstract into something more concrete. These practices allow you to "see" how the candidate thinks without dedicating half your morning to the effort.

PRACTICE:
NOTE-TAKING
FOR STRATEGY

Throughout this book we've emphasized the importance of a properly structured interview question. Assessing strategic thinking also requires a well-structured question. But the real secret isn't how you ask the question. It's how you take your notes.

Strategy is complex. Counter that by using what we've already discussed in a previous chapter—keep the question simple and open-ended and then use follow up questions.

> **Interviewer:** Think of a project you recently completed that required you to be strategic. Take a moment think of the project, let me know when you are ready.

> **Candidate:** Okay . . . sure . . . I'm ready.

Interviewer: Let's start by having you tell me the end goal of this project. Keep it as simple as possible, because I'm going to capture most of it in my notes.

The instructions to "keep it simple" keep the candidate focused and prevent them from going on too many tangents.

Candidate: The goal of the project was to create a new department focused on providing content expertise to clients, basically a group of in-house experts whose services we would provide as consultants.

This is where the importance of how you take notes will make all the difference. At the top of your notes, write the word "Goal" and jot their description down next to it, paraphrasing to capture the essence of the goal. Now ask a follow-up question for details:

Interviewer: Now let's talk about the resources available to help get to the end goal. Think of those any way you want. Budget, people, time, or anything else that was an input, whether you had complete control over them or not.

The prompt to think of "budget, people, time" is included because those are generally the resources people have during projects. At a minimum, you want to know those for this activity.

Candidate: We treated it like a startup. I had 100,000 dollars. I had two people on staff. We had three months to pull it together. I had a project plan from when it was last attempted . . . . I had backing from two very senior managers, that was a resource. Also, I had an initial client . . . and we had an internal repository of best-practices and white papers that we could leverage.

In your notes, beneath "Goal," label a section called "Resources." Each of the items they share should be written in that section

($100,000, 2 people, 3 months, project plan, 2 Sr. Managers, client, repository).

> **Interviewer:** Okay, let's get a few more things out. What were some of the potential obstacles or hurdles you were facing?

> **Candidate:** Well two of those things I mentioned as resources were also hurdles. We had a short timeline, only one client, also we hadn't identified which internal experts would be our consultants nor what method we would use to identify who would be good at this beyond just their expertise. We knew that their managers would object to this, and another issue was that the old project plan had nothing in it about marketing.

Now create a section called "Hurdles" in your notes. Each item they mention should go in that section (short timeline, 1 client, no identification of internal experts, no method for identifying, objection from managers, no marketing plan).

> **Interviewer:** Got it. And finally, tell me how it turned out. Let's keep that simple as well, no more than short synopsis.

> **Candidate:** It turned out great. We ended up with two internal experts who took on a project from the initial client. Before that was completed, we had three more clients, an internal structure for rotating experts through these projects so they could be spun out but then returned to their managers refreshed, and we had people lined up internally do take on more work. Since then we've had a steady stream of clients.

The candidate will almost always give you more than a synopsis. That is okay. Create a section called "Results" and paraphrase what they share to capture key points. Don't worry if you don't get all the details. Most of this exercise will be focused on the other sections of your notes. But letting them conclude the story gives you the full picture and gives them the satisfaction of closing it out.

This whole note-taking process should be done quickly. Your pacing should be fast, and it should take no more than three minutes. In doing so, you have visually recreated their project on your notepad:

Goal
Create a new department focused on providing content expertise to clients, basically a group of in-house experts whose services we would provide as consultants

Resources
$100,000, 2 people, 3 months, project plan, 2 Sr. Managers, client, repository

Hurdles
Short timeline, 1 client, no identification of internal experts, no method for identifying, objection from managers, no marketing plan

Results
2 internal experts took on a project from the initial client. Got three more clients. Created internal rotation so experts could spin out but return to manager refreshed. Lots of interest internally. Now has a steady stream of clients

Think of this note-taking structure as a chessboard with pieces. Just like chess, the ultimate game of strategy, you are going to start moving pieces around. Focus on the two pieces that will most illuminate their strategic thinking: resources and hurdles. Each of them will have a line of questioning that allows you to see how they think. Below are examples, but your actual questions will always be determined by the scenario they provide.

Resource Questions

There are two types of questions to ask about the resources. The first are probing questions on the resources themselves. You only need two or three of these brief follow-up questions. Keep the pace fast and the tone inquisitive. The purpose is to "see" how they thought about these resources:

- Let's begin with the resources. What was the purpose of bringing these two staff members onto the team? Did you have a choice? Who else could you have chosen? Why?
- How familiar were you with the repository? How big was it? Was it kept up to date well?
- How well did you know the two senior leaders?

After a few of the probing questions, move into the second type of questions which are "what-if-I-remove" questions:

- Of these resources listed, which was most important? . . . Okay, what if you didn't have access to that resource? How would that have changed things? What would you have done instead?
  - If the most important resource is something that can't be removed, such as the timeline, then simply make an adjustment to it. *"Okay, let's suppose the timeline was cut in half. How would that have changed things? What would you have done in that situation?"*

Repeat this line of questioning one or two more times, each time removing one of the resources but keeping the others on the table. *"Okay, let's suppose you had the same timeline, but no support from senior management, what do you do?"* Alternatively, rather than removing resources, you can make adjustments:

- What would you have done if you only had one person on your project?

- What if you only had half the budget?
- What if the repository was outdated?
- What if you had twice as much time to get it done? Half as much time?
- If you could have added another resource what would it have been?

Now that you have asked questions about Resources, move on to Hurdles and follow a similar protocol.

Hurdle Questions

With these questions, your notes only serve as visual references, helping with your questioning. Your questions should stay simple and focus on learning how they maneuvered around the hurdles they laid out:

- How did you identify the internal experts to leverage?
- How did you get around their managers objecting to releasing them for this work?
- What were some of your marketing ideas?

You can ask additional questions to gather an understanding of their ability to anticipate roadblocks:

- Which obstacle was unexpected? How did you manage it? Why did you not see it coming?
- Was there an obstacle you planned for, but ended up not having to deal with? Why was that?

As the interviewer, this activity should feel like watching a chess game. Pulling the project out of the candidate's mind and placing it in a structure in front of you allows you to easily see the board and the pieces. You can now move quickly, asking questions that matter, moving on from things that don't.

In a traditional interview, these questions would slow down the interview. While you will never be able to move at the speed of thought, your instructions to break the project apart along with your note-taking structure removes the need for them to access their memory and try to interpret it in the same moment. Now the strategic thinking, which you want to assess, will come through more clearly and your diagnosis will be more accurate.

PRACTICE:
SOLVE-IT

For some interviewers assessing strategy is difficult because they need more contextual information to know if the candidate made the right choices along the way. A great way to overcome this hurdle is to provide the candidate a real-life problem that you are trying to solve at work.

If you're worried about publicly sharing an internal problem you are trying to solve then instead make the assignment about a problem you have already solved. The problem should be given to them three or four days in advance. With the internet at everyone's disposal you don't have to prepare materials or share confidential organizational documents with them. Instead give them an assignment similar to the one below with the blank areas filled in by you with specifics from your organization:

> *You will discuss the following assignment with our team during your upcoming interviews next week.*
>
> One of our work streams/lines of business is "_____"
>
> What we do well is "_____"
>
> What we do *not* do well is "_____"
>
> Our problem is "_____"
>
> Here are some places online to learn more about this industry/ our organization/how others are addressing this/etc.: _____

During the interview we will spend 20 to 25 minutes discussing your solutions to our problem. The first 5 minutes will be dedicated to you asking us questions based on what you have learned so far. You can ask any question to better understand the problem, the history, the context, and so on. We will then use the remaining time to discuss your ideas for solving the problem.

Many interviewers balk at the idea of sending questions to candidates in advance. The traditional thinking is that a measure of a candidate's strength is their ability to answer questions on the spot. I agree that a candidate should be able to discuss their work experience without needing to know the questions in advance. I also agree with the theory that the first answer that comes to a candidate's mind is generally closest to the truth.

But you are doing neither of those when you are assessing strategic thinking. It is extremely rare that a person needs to be strategic in the moment. In fact, strategy, is far less about the current moment than it is about the ability to look ahead. Therefore, assessing strategy must be treated differently. *You want them to think in advance.* Strategy relies on thinking well and giving them time to think eliminates any excuses if their thinking isn't strong.

In fact, strategy, is far less about
the current moment than it is
about the ability to look ahead.

The first five minutes of the interview during which they ask you questions about the problem are the first window into their thinking. As they ask questions, gauge the sharpness of their questions.

- Are they asking questions that are relevant and help them understand the situation?
- Is it clear they prepared and aren't just asking questions they could have easily found online?

- Are they asking the questions your team has already asked as you tried to solve the problem? (That is a good thing.)
- Are they asking questions your team hasn't thought of? (That is even better).

Their questions tell you what they think is important, what mental paths they went down to solve the problem, and therefore *how* they think.

With the remaining fifteen to twenty minutes your goal is to create an environment where you can "see" how they think. To maximize this, you must follow a set of protocols.

First, don't criticize the candidate's ideas too quickly or forcefully. If you shut them down, you won't see *how* they think. By critiquing their ideas, you may learn how they react to pushback or under pressure, but that is a different assessment—don't confuse the two. It doesn't matter if they are going down a path that you've tried and know won't work. Let them continue. Never say, "That won't work." or "We tried that." If you do, you are missing the point of the exercise. Better responses are, "That is interesting. Why would we try that?" Or, "That one is complicated because we've run into this problem with that approach, how can we get around that?" You must keep the path open to see their thinking and push them along as necessary.

Second, offer ideas of your own. Strategy isn't just about original thinking but also being able to build on others' ideas. Make sure to join the conversation by asking questions such as:

- "What if we tried X? What do you think would happen?"
- "Given what you just said, I'm wondering if we should do X? Why do you think that?"

In doing this, avoid asking them explicitly about the quality of the options. For example, don't say, "What if we tried X? Good idea or bad idea?" If you ask it that way, the candidate will think there is a right or wrong answer and they will shift back into interview mode. You don't want them in interview mode—you want them in "thinking and discussing" mode. Using "Why do you think that?" and "What would happen?" drives broader strategic thinking as opposed to critical thinking which is triggered when judging.

Keep in mind you are not looking for the "right" answer. How they *get to the answer* is what allows you to assess strategy. Outlandish answers that indicate poor decisionmaking should hurt the candidate. But those are obvious to spot and you don't need to devote your mental energy to identifying them. I have seen many candidates land at a different decision than I would have, maybe even a wrong decision. But their thinking along the way was impressive enough to advance them. Rarely do final decisions get made in a vacuum, and even the best people make the wrong decisions, so the assessment shouldn't focus on their final decision.

Through this approach you will get a much better sense of the person's strategic ability than asking an "off-the-shelf" strategy question. In addition, you will gain a stronger sense of what it would be like to work and thought partner with them.

ADDITIONAL BENEFIT

A set of questions like those used to identify strategic thinking has the additional benefit of helping you to assess other skills or qualities. Since critical thinking is a subset of strategic thinking, you will certainly be able to assess it. But you will likely also have an opportunity to assess some of the other components of strategy—creativity, judgment, decisiveness, planning, and comfort with ambiguity. The odds are high that you will get a sense of their functional skills and role-specific knowledge along the way as well.

CONTINUOUS
IMPROVEMENT

ccording to the American Psychiatric Association (APA) "compulsions" are repetitive behaviors or mental acts that a person feels driven to perform in response to an obsession. "Obsessions" are recurrent and persistent thoughts, impulses, or images.[1] As stand-alone behaviors, the two are not necessarily negative. Even when found together, the consequences aren't necessarily a concern. The trouble occurs when the two together become time-consuming (more than one hour a day), cause major distress, and impair work, social, or other important functions. This is called obsessive-compulsive disorder (OCD) and impacts 1 to 3 percent of the population.

This condition has been studied for more than three centuries. In the seventeenth and eighteenth centuries the disorder was blamed on demons and spirits. In the nineteenth century, French clinicians began a more rigorous study of "folie du doute" or "doubting madness." Since then, modern research and understanding of the condition has been tied to psychological, biological, and evolutionary origins. Based on this research OCD appears to have roots in normal cognitive functioning and stems from adaptive behavior such as awareness of present and future threats.[2] This in turn allows the person to plan for and avoid potential threats.[3]

Considering the impairment that obsessive-compulsive disorder can have on affected individuals, it seems counterintuitive to find something positive in the condition. But neuroscientist Dr. Martin Bruene describes OCD as an extreme on a continuum of evolved harm-avoidance strategies.[4] According to the APA, many people have focused thoughts or repeated behaviors, and this can add structure or make tasks easier. Recognizing this as a cognitive continuum helps us identify a set of desirable traits and behaviors that lead to individual and organizational success.

If you want a high-performing organization then you want to hire people who are rarely satisfied with the current outcomes. What you want is a person who has a compulsion to make things better—but is in control. This quality, continuous improvement, is difficult to assess because it is both skill and traits. The skill is problem-solving. The traits involve a distaste for "good enough" or a reluctance to leave well enough alone and a striving for perfection.

The candidate must have a *distaste* for "good enough," coupled with knowing when "good enough" is enough. They must have the *reluctance* to leave well enough alone, not the *inability* to leave well enough alone. If they want every utensil in their kitchen drawer to be two centimeters apart, that's not a problem. If they can't leave their house until that is done, that is a problem. Similarly, if they want perfection at work, that's not an issue. If they can't move forward without it, that is an issue. It is the striving for perfection, not perfection itself that you want to identify.

To effectively assess for continuous improvement, you must assess problem-solving and the underlying compulsion to make things better—a controlled perfectionism. One approach is to assess for both. The other is to only assess for the underlying compulsion. The idea behind the second approach is that if a person truly has this compulsion, then they not only like improving things but have been doing it a long time and are therefore good at it. Because I favor effectiveness and efficiency, I prefer the second approach. But first, let's discuss problem-solving separately.

PROBLEM-SOLVING

One approach to assessing problem-solving is to interview like many technology companies do. Silicon Valley is infamous for their problem-solving questions. Examples of questions used in that industry can be found with a simple internet search:

- You have eight balls all the same size. Seven of them weigh the same, and one of them weighs slightly more. How can you find the ball that is heavier by using a balance and only two times to weigh?
- You are shrunk to the height of a nickel and your mass is proportionally reduced so as to maintain your original density. You are then thrown into an empty glass blender. The blades will start moving in sixty seconds. What do you do?

Consulting firms have the same reputation for asking hard problem-solving questions:

- How would you break down the cost of the pen in my hand?
- Estimate the revenue from the sale of tickets at the most recent Olympics.

If you need an insanely smart person on your team, then use these types of questions. If your organizational culture is one in which the insanely smart people rise into leadership positions, then these types of questions can be helpful. I believe leaders need to be a lot of things—insanely smart is not one of them. Just plain old smart will do.*

As much as I am a proponent for different approaches to interviewing, there are times when traditional methods are the best. If you don't need insane smarts, traditional problem-solving questions will do just fine. The following questions are straightforward behavioral questions and any subset of them can be used to gauge the candidate's skills:

- Describe a specific problem you solved at work.
  - How did you approach the problem?

---

* Leaders *do* need to have the judgment to determine which roles on their team need insane smarts and which don't.

- Who did you involve?
- What was the outcome?
- Have you ever had to solve a problem with limited information?
  - What information did you have?
  - How did you use the information?
  - What is an alternative solution you could have landed at with the same information?
- What is the most difficult problem you have had to solve at work, home, or school?
  - What was the outcome?
  - What did you learn from the experience?
- In a recent role, have you had to take on a problem that previously had not been addressed?
  - Why had it not been addressed?
  - What was your solution?
  - Was your solution adopted?

These are all great questions for assessing problem-solving and I've used each of them with much success. If you want to independently assess problem-solving, then use two of them coupled with at least two of the "controlled perfectionism" questions below. Together they will help you determine if the candidate has the continuous improvement disposition that is so valuable in any organization.

CONTROLLED PERFECTIONISM

When I used problem-solving questions like those above to gain insight on continuous improvement, I began to realize that they weren't giving me any new insight about the candidate that all my other "non-problem-solving" questions weren't already providing. In other words, all my other behavioral questions which began with "Have you ever had to . . ." also gave me a sense of the candidate's problem-solving ability. This was true whether the intended topic of the question was to assess relationship-building, project management, negotiating skills, or any other area of interest. They all contained an element of problem-solving. By the time the candidate had gone through an interview or two, problem-solving was already effectively assessed.

I don't like to waste time, which led me to focus on the compulsion to fix things as my primary assessment of continuous improvement. My recommendation is to skip questions specific to problem-solving and instead spend your time assessing controlled perfectionism.

Compulsions aren't easy to assess. Fortunately, they shine bright when uncovered, as is the case with controlled perfectionism. To begin, choose any two of the following questions.

- Has there been something at work that wasn't going well, and you worked to fix it?
    - What was the result?
    - Why did you take that on?
- Have you improved something recently at work?
    - What was the result?
    - Why did take that on?
- Have you recently initiated a change in a process or operation at work?
    - What was the result?
    - What made you take that on?
- Have you made any suggestions at work to improve the way job processes or operations work?
    - What was the result?
    - What made you raise the suggestion?
- Have you ever noticed something that was not getting done at work that was outside your area, but you still worked to get it done?
    - What was the result?
    - What made you take that on?

You'll notice all the questions have the same two follow-up questions. Those questions specifically address the compulsion you are seeking. You are looking for responses that contain any version of the following phrases:

- "I don't like things to be inefficient . . ."
- "I can't stand when something isn't working well . . ."
- "Stuff like that just bothers me . . ."
- "When something is broken, I fix it . . ."
- "I like figuring out how to make things better . . ."

You must stay in tune for this compulsion, because those seemingly innocuous phrases can get lost in the general answer. But those phrases are like diamonds covered in dirt, just barely noticed except by those who know to look for the glimmer. Asking about results is key because you also want to make sure their desire for things to be perfect doesn't become a bottleneck. Keep a cautious ear open for any version of the following responses because they could be flags for concern:

- "We pushed back the deadline a few times . . ."
- "I just decided to do it all myself . . ."

If their perfectionism is out of control, it can push them in the other direction and rather than taking too long or taking too much on, they don't complete anything. You should also raise a mental flag and note to yourself if the candidate gives responses with some element of:

- "I had to move on to another project, so I wasn't able to complete this one."
- "The amount of time it would have taken to get it right wasn't worth it."
- "The further I dug, I kept finding new problems, and there was just no end to it."

All these answers are legitimate answers, but the person you want to hire must consistently leave projects and problems better off than when they found them. If the candidate is leaving them in the same state as when they found them, then they are not in control of their compulsion—rather they are avoiding the fact that they couldn't get it perfect. Perhaps they are driven by the hunt, they tire if it isn't quickly solved, or they can't face not being perfect. The reasons for such behavior are too many to decipher and some may be valid. But if you hear these responses more than once, that is a warning sign. Make note of it, and if the candidate advances make sure you use the reference checks to learn if they are in control or not. The compulsion to improve only helps if things *do* improve.

In addition to picking two of the questions above, use two of the following to continue assessing if there is a compulsion for controlled perfection.

- Tell me a few things that you would consider pet peeves at work.
  - Why are those pet peeves?
- How much do small errors bother you? Give me an example?
  - Why did that stand out?
- On a scale of 1 to 10, how detail-oriented are you?
  - Give me an example that justifies that.
- Have you spent too much time on a project trying to get it right? Tell me about that experience.

The themes you are looking for are the same as with the previous questions. They should be bothered by things that are not right or are out of place. These things should not bother them so much that they can't move forward. The answers should display reasonable perfectionism, not irrational perfectionism. It should be clear they are in control of it, not controlled by it.

AFFECTION FOR PROBLEM-SOLVING

Another effective approach for assessing continuous improvement is to use the following question:

Interviewer: What type of problems are you uniquely good at solving? Give me an example for each.

This may sound like a traditional problem-solving question, but you aren't asking them to solve a problem, rather you are looking for an answer that demonstrates a genuine affection for problem-solving. People who like solving problems know what type of problems they like, and you can hear the joy they get from this work in their answer. For example:

> **Candidate:** I really like process improvements. If can figure out how to do something in less time or with less people or less money, that really gets me going. Those are problems where I just love to dig in.

Or . . .

> **Candidate:** I'm a data geek. Love spreadsheets. There is something about dumping my data in Excel and just tearing through it to find the answer I need. It is the place where I need to be careful not to get too deep in the weeds, but that is what gets me going.

The candidate should light up during these answers. They immediately know what problems intrigue them and the language they use shows their connection to the work. This is someone who loves solving problems, and therefore will be driven to keep making things better.

If the answer is less colorful, that isn't a flag, you'll just have to make sure to dig deeper and harder on the compulsion questions. For example, a candidate may answer:

> **Candidate:** I tend to lean toward process improvements. Those are ones where you can easily measure if you got it right, you've either saved time or money or a resource like people. I've gotten good at figuring out those types of problems.

That isn't a bad answer: You now know what they are good at. But you will always need to pair it with several of the other questions to determine the depth of their compulsion and the level of their control.

Whether its origins are psychological, biological, or evolutionary, the desire to shape and improve the world around us is part of our cognitive make-up. Determining the strength of a candidate's compulsion to improve is a worthwhile investment. When in command, it translates into a strong hire who can move work forward in a way that others cannot.

CREATIVITY

*S*imilar to MRG and their study on leadership effectiveness, IBM has also been researching the various aspects of talent needed to succeed. Since 2004, they've conducted a Global CEO Study every two years. Separately, since 1999, they've conducted an annual Global C-Suite Study based on conversations with over 12,000 executives worldwide. In addition, they've conducted a range of other studies with general managers and public sector leaders representing organizations of varying size in sixty countries and thirty-three industries. IBM's studies are the largest and most comprehensive of their kind. As in MRG's research, strategic thinking consistently holds a top spot. But beginning in 2010, another contender began to show up at or near the top of the list—creativity.[1]

IBM's research indicates that navigating an increasingly complex world requires the ability to think creatively. The complexity is due to a mix of new business models, global integration, growing expectations of corporate social responsibility, technology, and increasingly informed customers. Eighty percent of CEOs anticipate this increase in complexity, but only 49 percent believe their organizations and their people are prepared to deal with it. To succeed, their organizations need talent that see things differently than others. They need creative thinkers who can help move organizations in unanticipated and ultimately successful directions.

When you ask people to describe their own creativity, it is difficult for them to do so. Steve Jobs echoed this sentiment during an interview for *Wired* magazine in 1996:

> When you ask creative people how they did something, they feel a little guilty because they didn't really do it, they just saw something. It seemed obvious to them after a while.[2]

Most interview questions don't acknowledge this reality and instead ask candidates to give examples of creative solutions they've generated in their work experience. These types of questions focus primarily on ideas and the results, not on the process. Assessing results, however, requires an understanding of the candidate's context. A candidate may describe something that was creative within their context, but to you it may seem lackluster. Or it may seem creative but was actually par for the course.

This is a problem you cannot solve. Regardless of your understanding of the candidate's context, your opening question still needs to be a traditional one in which you learn about creative solutions the candidate has generated. Start by asking any of the following standard creativity questions.

- Have you had a project which required you to think "outside the box"?
  - If so, what ideas did you generate and what was the result?
- Have you come up with an innovative idea or solution recently at work?
  - If so, what resulted from the idea?
- Have you faced a problem at work that you solved in a unique way?
  - If so, what was the outcome?

Whether or not you have insight on the candidate's context, this question is still valuable because it sets the foundation for addressing the challenge that Steve Jobs identified. To truly assess creativity, you will need to ask questions that specifically help you understand the candidate's mental process.

Similar to strategy, creativity is harder to assess because it is a mind state that people enter to generate results.[3] It is often more recognizable when examined via the artistic creativity exhibited by musicians, poets, dancers, or other artists. For this reason, a considerable amount of research on creative mental processes has been done with artists. Fortunately, artistic creativity and the creativity needed in the working world are related. Studies have shown that whether a person is a chief operating officer or a sculptor, a similar mental shift occurs when they think creatively. Dr. Joel Lopata, a Professor of Psychology and Creativity at The Sheridan Institute of Technology and Advanced Learning, found that, "When artists—or people in general—work across domains . . . they are in what can be called a distinct creative mental space, which is distinct and different from a rational, logical, and analytical state."[4]

That cognitive commonality between artists and professionals holds the answer to effective assessment of creative thinking. Think about someone you know who is artistic. How would you describe them when it comes to their art? Think about how they approach their work and how they are able to do what they do.

- They care deeply about their work. They spend hours refining it. They rewrite it countless times, look at it from countless angles, and start over countless times.
- They're able to suspend judgment. While they are working, they put aside what others will think about their art. They believe in it, even if others don't.
- They work hard even though they don't know if others will like the end product. Only in the execution do they know if what they've created has an impact. If they get rejected, they try again.

Creativity is about caring deeply, suspending judgment, and being tenacious. It is this combination of mental qualities that you need to assess for. To accomplish this, you will ask a series of questions that build upon one another. The place to begin is identifying whether the candidate has an artistic side. If so, it heightens the odds that they can get into a creative mind state when not at work and can do the same while at work as well. The first question is straight to the point:

- Do you have an artistic talent or interest (draw, sculpt, knit, write, sing)?

If the answer to the question above is "no," ask one or both of the following:

- Have you built something by hand?
- Have you ever had an idea for an invention?

If the answer to any of these questions is affirmative, dig deeper to see where it goes. Ask one of the following questions.

- When you were working on/thinking about _____, what is it that kept you engaged?
- Why do you like doing _____?

Now ask a question to begin connecting their artistic creativity to work:

- Have you ever found that same feeling for something at work? If so, what was it?

Whether the initial answer about their artistic talent is affirmative or not, continue by using the following questions to assess their tenacity and whether they've had experiences where they cared deeply about the outcomes:

- Have you had a project or assignment at work that you cared deeply about? Why did you care so deeply? How did that affect you? What was the result?
- Has there been a project that caused you to either stay longer at work or come back to it later when you were home, but not because of a deadline you had to meet?

Then close out this set of questions with one or both of the following:

- When do you come up with your best ideas?
- How often do you have ideas that get shot down?
    - If the answer is, "All the time," ask: "Why is that?" "Why do you keep offering up ideas?"
    - If the answer is, "Rarely," ask: "Why is that?" "Tell me about an idea that did get shot down?"

Asking them when they come up with ideas helps you determine how invested they become in the creative process. The answer you want to hear are things like, "while driving my car," "in the shower," "in the middle of the night." In short, the combination of caring deeply and tenacity means when they are in creative state, their mind doesn't only think about solutions while at work. Their mental wheels continue turning until they strike upon an idea.

Throughout this series of questions, you are listening for evidence of their ability to suspend judgement, deal with doubt, and keep plugging away. The question about ideas getting shot down is designed to identify that directly. In their answer you will hear whether doubt or judgment weakens them or strengthens them. Creative minds rebound from doubt or use it to move forward. They don't stay weakened by it.

In total, you will ask six or seven questions. The idea behind the line of questions is to gain a sense of whether the candidate has the underlying characteristics of creativity and if they've applied them in a work setting.

Sometimes you will find candidates who were not able to leverage their creativity because their work environment was stifling. They will usually acknowledge that the environment was not conducive to creativity and may acknowledge they struggled as a result. That is okay, because if you are seeking creative thinking then you want someone who will be unhappy if they can't express that side of themselves through their work. That unhappiness is not a bad thing. It is often what propels them forward to change things and to make progress even if they are only allowed to tinker around the edges.

As the interviewer, you need to know how much creativity is ideal for the role. If you believe you need high levels of creativity, then you are looking for someone who will have answers during an interview that you hadn't prepared for. That means you need to know your own comfort with creativity. Because if *you* are less creative you will likely eliminate creative people. You will view them as hard to manage because they always want to try something new or "crazy."

If during the interview you think the candidate's answers are "too different," then withhold judgment and ask yourself, *"But isn't that what I want? Or is it too much?"* If the candidate's ideas are coupled with rigorous thinking, strong analytical skills, strong judgment, or any other criteria you have, then you shouldn't view the candidate negatively. Creatively pushing the envelope requires an element of risk-taking. And not just from the candidate, but from the person doing the hiring.

EMOTIONAL INTELLIGENCE
(CIRCA 1990)

*D*r. Peter Salovey is a psychologist, founder of Yale's Center for Emotional Intelligence and President of Yale University. Dr. John D. Mayer is a noted author on the topic of emotional intelligence, psychologist, and professor at the University of New Hampshire. Thirty years ago, Mayer and Salovey pioneered research on "emotional intelligence" as well as coined the term itself. They continue to be leaders in the field and their current perspective is quite interesting: Emotional intelligence is no longer a valid concept.

That's putting it gently. After seeing how the topic of their research had evolved over several decades, they published an article on emotional intelligence (EI).[1] Here are a few other ways they described its current usage:

> . . . there is widespread misuse of the term to apply to concepts that simply are not concerned with emotion or intelligence or their intersection . . .

> . . . only when researchers revert to using the term to refer to its legitimate meaning within the conceptual, scientific network can it be taken seriously. . .

. . . much of the research on EI can be referred to as a degenerating research program which consists of a series of defensive shifts in terminology and hypotheses unlikely to yield new knowledge or understanding. . .

My personal favorite from the article is when Mayer and Salovey suggest that part of the problem is the "exaggerated tenderness" among researchers in psychology and call for the approach of scholars in philosophy and law where "a dumb argument is called a dumb argument, and he who makes a dumb argument can expect to be slapped down by his peers."

To gain a better understanding of how things took such a turn, let's go back to the beginning. In 1990, Mayer and Salovey published an article called "Emotional Intelligence" in a journal entitled *Imagination, Cognition and Personality*.[2] Their framework contained "a set of skills hypothesized to contribute to the accurate appraisal and expression of emotion in oneself and in others, the effective regulation of emotion in self and others, and the use of feelings to motivate, plan, and achieve in one's life." Five years later, Dr. Daniel Goleman, a psychologist and journalist for *The New York Times*, wrote a book about the concept, also entitled *Emotional Intelligence*. The book became a bestseller and was on *The New York Times* Best-Seller List for a year and a half. Since then EI has grown into a full-blown industry of publications, testing, and consulting.

Mayer and Salovey believe that all the attention has led to a misunderstanding of EI and in their words, "we agree with many of our colleagues who have noted that the term emotional intelligence is now employed to cover too many things—too many different traits, too many different concepts."[3]

It's not that EI isn't a valid and powerful framework. Rather, new research has shined a more nuanced and critical light on the concept, and not enough people are listening. For example, the most commonly cited research on EI states that it accounts for 58 percent of success across a range of occupations and that 90 percent of top performers have high emotional intelligence.[4] But a more recent meta-analysis

analyzed hundreds of studies on the connection between job performance and EI.[5] This study found the link to be inconsistent and that
the value of EI depends on the job.

In some professions, such as sales or counseling, it helps. In others,
such as scientists and accountants, it hurts performance. Another study,
aptly titled "The Jekyll and Hyde of Emotional Intelligence," revealed
how people with high EI can also be more likely to engage in deviant
actions such a publicly embarrassing a co-worker.[6] A separate study had
similar results, showing how individuals high in EI may use their skills
to advance their own interests at the expense of others.[7] This newer
research indicates that the current usage of EI needs reexamination
before defining it as a hallmark of performance.

Mayer and Salovey believe that the framework has evolved too
much and has become too broad, rendering it ineffective. Goleman's
framework, the most renowned in the EI space, has no less than twelve
elements: self-awareness, emotional self-control, adaptability, achieve-
ment orientation, positive outlook, empathy, organizational awareness,
influence, coach and mentor, conflict management, teamwork, and
inspirational leadership. While that many elements may be helpful
from a development standpoint (i.e., as a tool for determining a current
employee's strengths and weaknesses), it is ineffective from a candidate
assessment standpoint.

Mayer and Salovey still believe in the power of their original work.
To safeguard the concept, they provide a set of five recommendations.
Central to their recommendations is a return to the simpler version
of emotional intelligence. Since 2002, The Broad Center has been
gathering data on the work performance of our program participants
through 360 feedback, supervisor feedback, executive coaching, and
a range of other evaluations and supports. The data, quantitative and
qualitative, aligns with Mayer and Salovey's perspective and points to
a narrowed definition of emotional intelligence as well: one that can
be successfully assessed and is far more useful during an interview.

Rather than attempting to assess EI through a wide range of traits
or qualities, I recommend focusing only on two; self-awareness and

empathy. Over the years, I've collected a set of questions that provide a deeper understanding of these two important characteristics.[*]

Rather than attempting to assess EI through a wide range of traits or qualities, I recommend focusing only on two; self-awareness and empathy.

SELF-AWARENESS

Self-awareness is the mechanism that allows us to gather and process information about ourselves. It helps us understand how we are perceived. With this in hand we can reflect on our own actions and, based on the situation, determine what is the appropriate or most-needed behavior or next step. Self-awareness helps us recognize when our own behavior is the cause of issues on a team or in a relationship. It enables the type of reflection needed to improve one's own performance. When paired with humility, it allows us to put what is good for the team above our own needs.

The questions to assess self-awareness do not all need to be asked, and there is no specific order. Experiment until you find the ones that work best for you.

- What do you think we think about you as a candidate?
    - *Follow-up:* What do you think is our "question mark" about you?

---

[*] I cannot claim the creation of all these questions. Some I created independently, some evolved out of questions I gathered along the way, and others were long ago borrowed from an article, conversation, book, or other source of inspiration. I share broad credit with the countless influences I have learned from.

Self-awareness: If the candidate can correctly describe how you perceive them, then that is a signal that they are aware of how they are perceived. The other strength of this question is that is sometimes causes the candidate to reveal a development area you were not previously aware of.

- To what do you attribute where you currently are in your career/ life?

Self-awareness (Humility): A good answer should acknowledge the benefit of external factors, e.g., help from others (mentors, teachers, parents), privilege, or even luck. A problematic answer is solely focused on internal factors such as "hard work," "intelligence," or other answers that indicate they believe they did it all on their own. There are some people who had no help in their lives. But even those people, if humble, recognize the external factors that impacted them.

- Are you currently where you thought you'd be in your career? Why or why not?

Self-awareness (Humility): Most people are not where they envisioned themselves to be in their careers. Being able to articulate why they aren't often provides insight on their ability to be self-reflective. This is also one that can provide perspective on their humility.

Note: Some people will answer that they are where they thought they would be. Their answer often reveals that the person is disciplined or a strong planner. My concern with this answer is that a person who is exactly where they thought they'd be may not have dealt with enough failure or setbacks. Their resilience hasn't been tested. I value resilience, and as a result it raises a slight flag for me to follow up on.

- Tell me about a professional accomplishment or goal that you have not achieved yet, but you should have by now? Why is that important? What is stopping you?

Self-awareness (Humility): Like the question above, a strong answer that acknowledges not meeting a goal will display humility and reflection.

- Share some recent feedback that you received that you did *not* agree with.

Self-awareness (Humility): Receiving feedback is hard to hear, particularly when it is true and hits a nerve. This question tends to reveal a development area candidates don't want to admit they have. Their tone in discussing it will reveal their openness to acknowledging their need to develop. How vehemently they disagree provides insight on their self-awareness and ego, particularly if your assessment so far suggests the feedback may be accurate.

- What is a common misperception about you?
  - *Follow-up:* What have you done to correct that misperception?
  - *Follow-up:* How has this gotten in the way of you getting things done?

Self-Awareness: This simple question is much more complex than it appears. In short, misperception is the same as perception, which we all know is reality. The difference is the candidate doubts that it is true. By asking this question you can learn what other people think about the candidate and whether the candidate is self-aware enough to not be in denial about it. Often candidates will realize the nuance of this question in the middle of answering. In those instances, you will witness them try to prove they aren't the way they are perceived. Sometimes they are able to provide a legitimate answer, other times it is clear they are only deceiving themselves. The follow-up questions allow you to learn if the candidate can self-regulate and change their behavior. If they are self-aware and self-regulate, they will share specific things they have done to change the initial perception of them.

EMPATHY

The concept of empathy has its roots in philosophy rather than psychology. It originated in Germany in the 1870's where it first appeared in philosopher Robert Vischer's Ph.D. dissertation as the word "einfuhlung" or "feeling into."[8] It described a person's capacity to experience a piece of art or literature and feel the emotions of the artist. Theodore Lipps, a German professor and philosopher, further developed the concept into a framework describing the ability to identify with another person. His work lead to a new branch of interdisciplinary research which combined psychology and philosophy. By the early 1900s the concept had moved west, and psychologist Edward Titchener is credited with naming it "empathy."

In this sense, empathy is like a sibling to self-awareness. While self-awareness is about understanding yourself, empathy is understanding how others are feeling. It allows you to see things from their perspective. From a professional perspective this is important because you can then anticipate the effect of your actions or decisions on others. Empathy has been linked not only to stronger leadership, but also to being perceived by others as a strong leader.[9]

Similar to self-awareness, the questions used to assess empathy do not all need to be asked and there is no specific order. Experiment until you find the ones that work best for you.

- Describe a work relationship with someone you did not particularly get along with.
  - *Follow-up:* Why did they act that way?

Empathy: The initial question primarily gives you context; it is the follow-up question that allows you to determine the candidate's ability to empathize. Despite the poor relationship, if they have empathy, they can still put themselves in another person's shoes and describe that person's point of view. They should be able to describe why that person may exhibit the behavior they did, even if that explanation implies that the candidate was at fault in some way. Whether they agree with the other person's perspective is not important,—what's important is that they can acknowledge the other person's perspective and show an understanding of it.

- Describe a time that you worked with someone who was very different from you.
  - *Follow-up:* Were you able to find a way to work with them?

Empathy (Self-Awareness): This question is very similar to the preceding question, however, it often provides an additional piece of valuable information. By describing a person who is different from them, the candidate sheds light on themselves. For example, the candidate may answer, "She was really detail-oriented and needed every step documented." This tells me that the candidate in front of me is not on that end of the spectrum.

Most candidates realize, sometimes midway through, that they are revealing something about themselves as well and try to rectify it. *"Not that I'm not detail-oriented, I understand the value of details. I'm just saying that she was really, really detail-oriented, almost in a bad way. . ."* If the candidate lacks self-awareness, they won't realize that they are revealing themselves. The candidate without self-awareness doesn't try to rectify it, they just continue to indict themselves. The dual value of this question is that it can also flag self-awareness as a concern.

- If someone has a strong opinion on something, how would you convince them otherwise if your opinion is different?

Empathy: An average to good answer is one in which the candidate explains how they would explain and garner support for their viewpoint. The answer will likely rely on finding evidence (data, historic proof, successful comparisons, etc.) to back their viewpoint. It may also include finding others to champion their viewpoint, particularly if those champions have a good relationship with the person they are trying to convince. The clarity, persuasiveness, and believability of their approach will impact the quality of this answer. A great answer may include all this, but it won't end there. A person with a strong empathetic foundation will spend time understanding the other person's viewpoint. They will want to understand why the other person's opinion is so strong and why they haven't been convinced before. Once they know this, they will then take the aforementioned approaches and mold them to best address the drivers of the opinionated person.

- What does it take to deliver bad news well?

Empathy: A poor answer is one in which the candidate suggests just sticking to the facts they need to deliver. If they lead only with logic and rationale, but don't acknowledge any emotional aspect that they need to consider, they lack empathy. They should acknowledge that depending on the type of news delivered, they should prepare for an emotional reaction (anger, sadness, shock) and their job is to remain calm. This doesn't mean they shouldn't be direct. Being candid is the best way to deliver bad news. But if they have empathy, they know to pair it with compassion.

"SCORING" EMOTIONAL INTELLIGENCE

Although the questions provided above will help assess emotional intelligence, they won't be enough. During an interview process, you are assessing candidates on two broad categories—skills and qualities.* Skills are what the candidate can do. Qualities are how they do what they do. Budgeting is a skill. Self-awareness and empathy are qualities. Subjectivity when assessing qualities is far higher than when assessing skills. This must be managed carefully to get an accurate assessment.

Each of us has had our own experiences which have shaped how we view the world. We see other people through the filter of our experiences. This means qualities like self-awareness and empathy will be

---

* Qualities are sometimes referred to as traits, personality traits, attributes, or characteristics.

judged relative to our own self-awareness and empathy. If you are a very empathetic person, you will judge an answer differently than an interviewer who is far less empathetic. Therefore, when assessing qualities like self-awareness, empathy, or any other, have everyone assess for the qualities.

Everyone? Yes. Everyone.

For qualities to be accurately assessed they must be viewed by multiple people and in multiple contexts. It is rare that you will know if someone is emotionally intelligent from one interaction. There are many instances in life when we learned someone was different than we first assumed. In life, you can get to know people and correct those assumptions. With candidates you have a limited number of opportunities.

> For qualities to be accurately
> assessed they must be
> viewed by multiple people
> and in multiple contexts.

In addition to the questions specific to self-awareness and empathy, implement a process that captures what all the other interviewers *sense about the candidate throughout the entire interview process.* Creating a process to capture what people sense may sound counterintuitive, but the form below is designed to do just that.

Qualities	Didn't Notice	Did Notice	Potential Issue
Self-Awareness			
Empathy			
Another quality			
Another quality			
Etc. . . .			

Here is how you use the tool. In the left column, list self-awareness, empathy, and any other qualities needed for your role. The effectiveness of this tool relies on strict adherence to a set of instructions:

- This form should be the last page of *every* question packet given to your interviewers. Even for interviews whose focus is *not* self-awareness nor empathy.
- *Every* interviewer who interviews the candidate has this form with them *every* time they interview. If Interviewer A interviews the candidate on Monday, they fill out this form based on that interaction. If the candidate interviews again on Friday and Interviewer A sees them again, they fill out another form again.
- At the end of each interview, interviewers independently assesses if they noticed any of the qualities. This is not a score, just a method for tracking what was sensed.
- If they *did* notice a quality (regardless to which degree) they check "Did Notice."
- If the interviewer did *not* notice a quality, they check "Did Not Notice." This is not considered a negative. Qualities are not consistently noticed. Rarely does a candidate exhibit all the desired qualities in one sitting, if ever. This instruction is important so interviewers know it is fine to mark "Did Not Notice."
- If the interviewer notices the *opposite* of a quality (e.g. "apathy," "lack of self-awareness," etc.) they should mark "Potential Issue."
- Interviewers shouldn't share their assessments with each other during the interview so they don't influence what others sense.

After the candidate has completed their interviews for the day, the interviewers discuss what they sensed during a debrief. What you are looking for are trends. These qualities were independently assessed at different points, so trends are much more likely to be valid.

- If a quality shows up as "Did Notice" twice or more, chances are the person has that quality. That doesn't mean to stop looking for it. It just means you are starting to see evidence of it.
- If a quality shows up as "Did Not Notice" consistently across interviewers, that is not a bad indicator. The candidate may be more reserved or doesn't easily show that side of themselves. Use the questions specific to self-awareness and empathy to specifically assess the qualities and continue using the tool in the following interviews to continue gathering evidence.
- If the candidate has any qualities marked as "Potential Issues," you will want to discuss what behavior drove those indications. It is possible the candidate does not have these qualities at the level you need. Continue to use the tool throughout the process to gather more evidence in either direction.

The interesting thing about qualities is that their negative version, when present, is more easily noticed. For example, lack of self-awareness is easier to notice than self-awareness. Arrogance is easier to notice than humility. Therefore, while it can be difficult to identify strengths in emotional intelligence, people who lack the qualities are easily identified with this process.

WORDS OF CAUTION

Two words of caution about this practice. First, although qualities are more valid after multiple assessments in multiple contexts, that does not imply that a single assessment isn't valid. If an interviewer senses that a candidate lacks emotional intelligence, but the process hasn't flagged it as an issue—the interviewer should still express that concern. You have enough mechanisms to gather evidence and discuss it, even if others don't feel the same way. It is better that an individual interviewer airs concern. The team can then decide to probe specifically in the next round while still using the tool to gather evidence.

The second word of caution is that if your interviewers are not diligent about tracking what they sense with the tool, you will have no data to work with. To make things tougher, there are times when your interviewers are diligent, but the candidate is hard to read, so you still end up with forms on which the "Did Not Notice" box is consistently checked off. When this happens, don't be discouraged or lose faith in the system. Keep in mind that same result would have happened without the system for that candidate anyway. There is always the candidate who is much harder to read and by the end of the day the interviewers are sitting around a table not quite sure about the qualities you were trying to assess.

This system won't always fix that. What it will fix is all the other times when interviewers are arguing about a candidate's "personality" because there was no process for independently gathering data, compiling it, and as a group seeing what it reveals.

Specifically assessing the narrowed definition of emotional intelligence in partnership with capturing what your interviewers sense in multiple contexts leads to more accurate decisions. That accuracy may result in more people on your team with strong emotional intelligence or fewer people without it. Either outcome is a win.

SELF-PURIFICATION

*W*hy is interviewing hard? Why aren't the odds in our favor to begin with? When I first began interviewing, I was constantly searching for resources to improve my accuracy. My desk was filled with books on interviewing, pages dog-eared, paragraphs highlighted. Articles on hiring best practices were an arm's reach away. My browser was filled with links to "best interview questions." But it wasn't enough. I was gaining experience and still making hiring mistakes. But why?

The lack of answers bothered me. I kept digging. An article would lead to an author, to a book, to a footnote, to an obscure reference, to another article, to a study. Every time I plunged down one of those rabbit holes, I inevitably landed face-first in one scientific journal or another. It was in this pursuit that I began to learn about cognitive science and first came across the work of psychologists Daniel Kahneman and Amos Tversky.

Kahneman and Tversky met while working at Hebrew University in Jerusalem and began conducting research together in the area of decisionmaking and judgment. Their research found that our thinking often deviates from the rationality one would expect. Effective decisionmaking is about the choices we make amid uncertainty. Kahneman and Tversky demonstrated that not only are those choices often irrational, but the systematic mental errors we make are specific and predictable.

In 1984, Tversky received the MacArthur "Genius Grant" for their work in cognitive science. In 2002, Kahneman received the Nobel Prize. The impact of their work continues to spread beyond psychology. Kahneman's bestselling book, *Thinking, Fast and Slow*, captures lessons from much of their research and has sold over 1.5 million copies. The recognition that our decisionmaking behavior can be anticipated and improved has been applied in nearly every setting where the odds are uncertain and people struggle to manage risk. Its fingerprints can be found in medicine, law, economics, public policy, finance, and most branches of social science.

The more I studied and the more I interviewed, the clearer it became that I, too, was trying to beat uncertain odds. I realized that when a candidate and an interviewer sit across the table from one another, they represent a struggle. A struggle to minimize risk. A struggle to understand. A struggle to make the right decision. A struggle to obtain the truth. During that struggle, the enemy is not the candidate. The cognitive sciences have taught us a lesson that political cartoonist Walt Kelly already knew many decades prior – the enemy is us.

That realization gave rise to another question. How do you overcome an internal struggle when you are your own worst enemy? And into the rabbit holes I plunged again. One of those holes deposited me into the writings of another great thinker. But this time it was neither a researcher nor a scientist. It was a practitioner. A leader who took risks and beat odds that few dare to face.

Stored in the archives of Stanford University's School of Humanities and Sciences is a draft of Martin Luther King Jr.'s "Letter from a Birmingham Jail." The letter, dated April 16, 1963, was penned by King as he sat in solitary confinement in the Birmingham City Jail.

King had arrived in Birmingham on April 2 to help direct a nonviolent campaign against segregation and other injustices. He began by leading a coordinated series of sit-ins, marches, and other peaceful demonstrations. On April 12, King and several others were arrested and jailed for their actions. Shortly thereafter, eight local clergy members issued a statement declaring that segregation in Alabama wasn't King's business and that he should leave.

King spent a week in solitary confinement. During this time, he wrote the now famous letter that captured his response to those clergy members. The letter—which contains the celebrated quote "Injustice anywhere is a threat to justice everywhere"—draws equally from the bible, T. S. Eliot, St. Augustine, and Socrates. Near the end of the second page, King lays out a set of principles for leading with non-violence:

> In any nonviolent campaign there are four basic steps: collection of the facts to determine whether injustices are alive, negotiation, self-purification, and direct action.

On this list, self-purification seems out of place. Too ethereal to be among the other tangible items. But historians view it differently. Self-purification was strategic, practical, and effective.

From the beginning of his work in civil rights, King studied Mahatma Gandhi's strategies for successfully leading India's independence movement against the British. One of Hinduism's foundational concepts is an enlightened state of self-consciousness called Brahman. To reach this state, Hinduism places emphasis on cleansing and purifying oneself. For Gandhi, the cleansing of anger, selfishness, and violence from one's heart and mind was essential to preparing for a struggle. For non-violence to succeed, protesters subjected to violence during a demonstration had to be mentally prepared to not respond in kind. When attacked, the natural reaction is to give up or retaliate. That instinct had to be controlled.

King adapted Gandhi's methods and the principle of self-purification made its way into King's principles. In India, self-purification included prayer, fasting, meditation, or yoga. In the U.S., civil rights leaders led workshops, role-plays, and discussions. Demonstrators were trained to be aware of and manage their first reactions and respond differently than they normally would. It was critical that the world see the demonstrators' resolve, but also that the world see the contrast between peace and violence. Self-purification had its roots in spirituality. In practice it was a powerful strategy grounded in mental preparation.

In all my years of working with leaders across the country, a distinguishing feature of the strongest ones is their mental preparation.

They know that in any struggle, if you simply react and aren't mentally prepared, the odds are against you. Because of their introspection, they overcome flawed thinking, consistently make the right decisions, and accomplish greatness. King and Gandhi understood this as they prepared before demonstrations. Kahneman and Tversky saw it as they ran study after study. From boardrooms to corporate hallways to classrooms to meeting rooms to interview rooms to any setting where decisions must be made, instinct and good fortune are not enough.

In its purest form, that is what this book is about. It is a set of principles and practices that allow you to prepare for the mental struggle that an interview is—a struggle that you only have a 50 percent chance of winning. The book is based on science and research. It is based on years of interviewing. It is based on days upon days of sitting next to great interviewers. I know firsthand it is a struggle you can win. But only if you mentally prepare.

Mental preparation serves as a foundational tenet for every practice in this book. All the hard work of understanding the person across the table can be undone without an understanding of yourself. Don't rush into the interview room, crumpled question packet in hand. Pause. Take responsibility. Note your first impressions. Manage your body language. Reword the question. Build trust. Let the question breathe. Be mindful. Know your target. Pause. Prepare.

All the hard work of understanding
the person across the table
can be undone without an
understanding of yourself.

It is my hope that the growth and introspection you gain from this book moves beyond the interview room, beyond your professional life, and develops you as a person as well. If not, may it at least help you shift the odds away from a coin toss and toward great talent.

ACKNOWLEDGMENTS

*I*f we've ever sat next to each other in an interview room, then I've learned from you. If we've discussed interviewing, I've learned from you. If we've recruited together, posted jobs, hosted webinars, reviewed resumes, read applications, watched candidate videos, wrote interview questions, designed rubrics, created protocols, built systems, participated in debriefs, agonized over hiring decisions and everything in between—I've learned from you.

We search for talent. We take chances. We give second chances. We keep the bar high. We question ourselves. We trust each other. We succeed. We fail. We laugh. We pound the table. We speak the unspoken. We fight for those not in the room. We make a difference. Always, I learn from you.

Too many lessons to name. So many people to honor. You know who you are. To one and all, thank you.

NOTES

Introduction

1. Frank L. Schmidt and John E. Hunter. "The Validity and Utility of Selection Methods in Personnel Psychology: Practical and Theoretical Implications of 85 years of Research Findings." *Psychological Bulletin* 124, no. 2 (1998): 262–274.
2. ERE Recruiting Intelligence. "Ouch, 50% Of New Hires Fail! 6 Ugly Numbers Revealing Recruiting's Dirty Little Secret." https://www.ere.net/ouch-50-of-new-hires-fail-6-ugly-numbers-revealing-recruitings-dirty-little-secret/.
3. Gallup. "Why Great Managers Are So Rare." https://www.gallup.com/workplace/231593/why-great-managers-rare.aspx
4. U.S. Department of Labor, Bureau of Labor Statistics. https://www.bls.gov/news.release/tenure.nr0.htm.

Strategy 1

1. Scott Highhouse. "Stubborn Reliance on Intuition and Subjectivity in Employee Selection." *Society for Industrial and Organizational Psychology* 1, no. 3 (September 2008): 333–342.
2. Nalini Ambady and Robert Rosenthal. "Half a Minute: Predicting Teacher Evaluations from Thin Slices of Nonverbal Behavior and Physical Attractiveness." *Journal of Personality and Social Psychology* 64, no. 3 (March 1993): 431–441.
3. Rachel E. Frieder, Chad H. Van Iddekinge, and Patrick H. Raymark. "How Quickly Do Interviewers Reach Decisions? An Examination of Interviewers' Decision-making Time Across Applicants." *Journal of Occupational and Organizational Psychology* 89, no. 2 (June 2016): 223–248.
4. Gary Klein. *Sources of Power.* The MIT Press, 1999.
5. Adrian Furnham and Hua Chu Boo. "A Literature Review of the Anchoring Effect." *Journal of Behavioral and Experimental Economics* 40, no. 1 (February 2011): 35–42; Raymond S. Nickerson. "Confirmation

Bias: A Ubiquitous Phenomenon in Many Guises." *Review of General Psychology* 2, no. 2 (1998): 175–220.

Strategy 2

1. Cynthia L. Picket, Wendi L. Gardner, and Megan Knowles. "Getting a Cue: The Need to Belong and Enhanced Sensitivity to Social Cues." *Personality and Social Psychology Bulletin* 30, no. 9 (September 1, 2004): 1095–1107.
2. Erik J. Schlicht, Shinsuke Shimojo, Colin F. Camerer, Peter Battaglia, Ken Nakayama. "Human Wagering Behavior Depends on Opponents' Faces." PLoS ONE 5, no. 7 (2010): https://doi.org/10.1371/journal.pone.0011663.

Strategy 3

1. Charles F. Bond and Bella M. DePaulo, Jr. "Accuracy of Deception Judgments." *Personality and Social Psychology Review* 10, no. 3 (August 1, 2006): 214–234.
2. Leanne ten Brinke. "Some Evidence for Unconscious Lie Detection." *Psychological Science* 25, no. 5 (May 1, 2014): 1098–1105.
3. https://admin.ks.gov/offices/personnel-services/recruitment/behavioral -interview-generator.

Strategy 4

1. Augustus A. White III and Beauregard Stubblefield-Tave. "Some Advice for Physicians and Other Clinicians Treating Minorities, Women, and Other Patients at Risk of Receiving Health Care Disparities." *Journal of Racial and Ethnic Health Disparities* 4, no. 3 (June 2017): 472–479.

Strategy 5

1. Mathias Leuthi, Beat Meier, and Carmen Sandi. "Stress Effects on Working Memory, Explicit Memory, and Implicit Memory for Neutral and Emotional Stimuli in Healthy Men." *Frontiers in Behavioral Neuroscience* 2, no. 5 (February 2008): https://doi.org/10.3389 /neuro.08.005.2008.
2. Travis J. Carter and David Dunning. "Faulty Self-Assessment: Why Evaluating One's Own Competence Is an Intrinsically Difficult Task." *Social and Personality Psychology Compass* 2, no. 1 (2008): 346–360.

Strategy 6

1. Martin Turner and Jamie Barker. *What Business Can Learn From Sport Psychology: Ten Lessons for Peak Professional Performance.* Bennion Kearny Limited, 2014.

2. Hendrie Weisinger and J. P. Pawliw-Fry. *Performing Under Pressure: The Science of Doing Your Best When It Matters Most.* Crown Business, 2015.

3. Don Compos. "The Interrogation of Suspects Under Arrest." *Studies in Intelligence* 2, no. 3 (July 1996): available at https://www.cia.gov /library/center-for-the-study-of-intelligence/kent-csi/vol2no3/html /v02i3a08p_0001.htm.

4. Luciano Bernardi, Camillo Porta, and Peter Sleight. "Cardiovascular, Cerebrovascular, and Respiratory Changes Induced by Different Types of Music in Musicians and Non-musicians: The Importance of Silence." *Heart* 92, no. 4 (2006): 445–452.

Strategy 7

1. Johanna M. Jarcho, Elliot T. Berkman, Matthew D. Lieberman. "The Neural Basis of Rationalization: Cognitive Dissonance Reduction During Decision-making." *Social Cognitive and Affective Neuroscience* 6, no. 4 (September 1, 2011): 460–467.

2. Gary Klein. "Performing a Project Premortem." *Harvard Business Review.* September 2007.

Strategy 8

1. Pamela Babcock. "Spotting Lies." *SHRM HR Magazine.* October 1, 2013.

2. Charles F. Bond and Bella M. DePaulo, Jr. "Accuracy of Deception Judgments." *Personality and Social Psychology Review* 10, no. 3 (August 1, 2006): 214–234.

3. Bogdan Wojciszke. "Multiple Meanings of Behavior: Construing Actions in Terms of Competence or Morality." *Journal of Personality and Social Psychology* 67, no. 2 (1994): 222–232.

4. John D. Teasdale, Barbara H. Dritschel, Melanie J. Taylor, Linda Proctor, Charlotte A. Lloyd, Ian Nimmo-Smith, and Alan D. Baddeley. "Stimulus-independent Thought Depends on Central Executive Resources." *Memory & Cognition* 23, no. 5 (September 1995): 551–559.

5. Matthew A. Killingsworth and Daniel T. Gilbert. "A Wandering Mind Is an Unhappy Mind." *Science* 330, no. 6006 (November 12, 2010): 932.

Strategy 9

1. Sarah Baker and Rosalind Edwards. *How Many Qualitative Interviews is Enough?* National Centre for Research Methods. 2012. available at http://eprints.ncrm.ac.uk/2273/4/how_many_interviews.pdf.

Strategy 10

1. Google. re:Work. Guide: Raise Awareness About Unconscious Bias. https://rework.withgoogle.com/guides/unbiasing-raise-awareness/steps/watch-unconscious-bias-at-work/.
2. Facebook. Managing Unconscious Bias. https://managingbias.fb.com/.
3. Starbucks Channel. *The Third Place: Our Commitment Renewed.* May 29, 2018. https://starbuckschannel.com/thethirdplace/.
4. Frank Dobbin and Alexandra Kalev. "Why Diversity Programs Fail." *Harvard Business Review.* July/August 2016; Patrick Forscher, Calvin Lai, Jordan Axt, Charles Ebersole, Michelle Herman, Patricia Devine, and Brian Nosek. "A Meta-Analysis of Procedures to Change Implicit Measures." *PsyARXiv Preprints* (August 13, 2018), available at https://psyarxiv.com/dv8tu/.
5. Jonathan S. Abramowitz, David F. Tolin, and Gordon P. Street. "Paradoxical Effects of Thought Suppression: A Meta-analysis of Controlled Studies." *Clinical Psychology Review* 21, no. 5 (July 2001): 683–703.
6. Gus Lubin and Shana Lebowitz. "58 Cognitive Biases That Screw Up Everything We Do." *Business Insider,* October 29, 2015. https://www.businessinsider.com/cognitive-biases-2015-10.
7. Lisa Legaut, Jennifer N. Gutsell, and Michael Inzlicht. "Ironic Effects of Antiprejudice Messages: How Motivational Interventions Can Reduce (but Also Increase) Prejudice." *Psychological Science* 22, no. 12 (November 28, 2011): 1472–1477.
8. Frank Dobbin and Alexandra Kalev. "Why Diversity Programs Fail." *Harvard Business Review.* July/August 2016.
9. David D. Burns. *Feeling Good: The New Mood Therapy.* Harper, 2008.
10. Emily Pronin, Daniel Y. Lin, and Lee Ross. "The Bias Blind Spot: Perceptions of Bias in Self Versus Others. *Personality and Social Psychology Bulletin* 28, no. 3 (March 1, 2002): 369–381
11. Amos Tversky and Daniel Kahneman. "Judgment under .Uncertainty: Heuristics and Biases." *Science* 185, no. 4157 (September 27, 1974): 1124–1131.

Strategy 11

1. Adam Luke and Bryan Gibson. "Mindfulness Meditation Reduces Implicit Age and Race Bias: The Role of Reduced Automaticity of Responding." *Social Psychological and Personality Science* 6, no. 3 (November 24, 2014): 284–291.

2. Irene V. Blair, John F. Steiner, and Edward P. Havranek. "Unconscious (Implicit) Bias and Health Disparities: Where Do We Go from Here?" *The Permanente Journal* 15, no. 2 (April 2011): 71–78.

3. Diana J. Burgess, Mary Catherine Beach, and Somnath Saha. "Mindfulness Practice: A Promising Approach to Reducing the Effects of Clinician Implicit Bias on Patients." *Patient Education and Counseling* 100, no. 2 (February 2017): 372–376.

4. Diana J. Burgess, Michelle van Ryn, John Dovidio, and Somnath Saha. "Reducing Racial Bias Among Health Care Providers: Lessons from Social-Cognitive Psychology." *Journal of General Internal Medicine* 22, no. 6 (June 2007): 882–887.

5. Beth Azar. "IAT: Fad or Fabulous?" *Monitor on Psychology* 39, no. 7 (July/August 2008): 44.

6. Claude M. Steel. *Whistling Vivaldi: How Stereotypes Affect Us and What We Can Do.* W.W. Norton & Company, 2011; Mahzarin Bahnaji and Anthony Greenwald. *Blind Spot: Hidden Biases of Good People.* Delacorte Press, 2013.

Strategy 12

1. John A. Byrne. "The Man Who Invented Management." *Bloomberg Businessweek*, November 27, 2005.

2. Colin Silverthorne. "The Impact of Organizational Culture and Person-Organization Fit on Organizational Commitment and Job Satisfaction in Taiwan." *Leadership & Organization Development Journal* 25, no. 7 (2004): 592–599; Sinisa Mitic, Jelena Vukonjanski, Edit Terek, Bojana Gligorovic, and Katarina Zoric. "Organizational Culture and Organizational Commitment: Serbian Case." *Journal of Engineering Management and Competitiveness* 6, no. 1 (2016): 21–27; Indira R. Guzman and Jeffrey M. Stanton. "IT Occupational Culture: The Culture Fit and Commitment of New Information Technologists." *Information Technology & People* 22, no. 2 (2009): 157–187.

3. John P. Meyer, Tracy D. Hecht, Harjinder Gill, and Laryssa Toplonytsky. "Person–Organization (Culture) Fit and Employee Commitment Under

Conditions of Organizational Change: A Longitudinal Study." *Journal of Vocational Behavior* 76, no. 3 (June 2010) 458–473.

4. Stuart Albert, Blake E. Ashforth, and Jane E. Dutton. "Organizational Identity and Identification: Charting New Waters and Building New Bridges." *The Academy of Management Review* 25, no. 1 (January 2000): 13–17.

5. Indira R. Guzman and Jeffrey M. Stanton. "IT Occupational Culture: The Culture Fit and Commitment of New Information Technologists." *Information Technology & People* 22, no. 2 (2009): 157–187.

6. Amy L. Kristof-Brown, Ryan D. Zimmerman, and Erin C. Johnson. "Consequences of Individuals' Fit at Work: A Meta-analysis of Person-Job, Person-Organization, Person-Group, and Person-Supervisor fit." *Personnel Psychology* 58, no. 2 (June 2005): 281–342.

7. Robert D. Beretz Jr., Sara L. Rynes, and Barry A. Gerhart. "Recruiter Perceptions of Applicant Fit: Commonalities and Differences." *Cornell University ILR School, DigitalCommons@ILR* (January 1992), available at https://digitalcommons.ilr.cornell.edu/cgi/viewcontent.cgi?referer= https://www.google.com/&httpsredir=1&article=1284&context=cahrswp.

Strategic Thinking

1. Robert Kabacoff. Develop Strategic Thinkers Throughout Your Organization. *Harvard Business Review.* February 7, 2014.

Continuous Improvement

1. American Psychiatric Association. "What Is Obsessive-Compulsive Disorder?" July 2017. https://www.psychiatry.org/patients-families/ocd /what-is-obsessive-compulsive-disorder

2. James F. Leckman and Michael H. Bloch. "A Developmental and Evolutionary Perspective on Obsessive-Compulsive Disorder: Whence and Whither Compulsive Hoarding?" *The American Journal of Psychiatry* 165, no. 10 (October 2008): 1229–1233.

3. David Mataix-Cols, Maria Conceição do Rosario-Campos, and James F. Leckman. "A Multidimensional Model of Obsessive-Compulsive Disorder." *The American Journal of Psychiatry* 162, no. 2 (February 2005): 228–238.

4. Martin Brune. "The Evolutionary Psychology of Obsessive-Compulsive Disorder: The Role of Cognitive Metarepresentation." *Perspectives in Biology and Medicine* 49, no. 3 (2006): 317–329.

Creativity

1. IBM. "IBM 2010 Global CEO Study: Creativity Selected as Most Crucial Factor for Future Success." May 18, 2010. https://www-03.ibm.com/press/us/en/pressrelease/31670.wss.

2. Gary Wolf. "Steve Jobs: The Next Insanely Great Thing." *Wired*, February 1, 1996.

3. Nancy C. Andreasen. "A Journey into Chaos: Creativity and the Unconscious." *MSM Mens Sana Monographs* 9, no. 1 (Jan/Dec 2011): 42–53.

4. Joel A. Lopata, Elizabeth A. Nowicki, and Marc F. Joanisse. "Creativity as a Distinct Trainable Mental State: An EEG Study of Musical Improvisation." *Neuropsychologia* 99 (May 2017): 246–258.

Emotional Intelligence

1. John D. Mayer, Peter Salovey, and David R. Caruso. "Emotional Intelligence: New Ability or Eclectic Traits?" *American Psychologist* 63, no. 6 (September 2008): 503–517.

2. Peter Salovey and John D. Mayer. "Emotional Intelligence." *Imagination, Cognition and Personality* 9, no. 3 (March 1, 1990): 185–211.

3. Mayer, Salovey, and Caruso. "Emotional Intelligence." 503–517.

4. TalentSmart. "About Emotional Intelligence." 2019. http://www.talentsmart.com/about/emotional-intelligence.php; Travis Bradberry. "Emotional Intelligence—EQ." *Forbes.com*, January 9, 2014. https://www.forbes.com/sites/travisbradberry/2014/01/09/emotional-intelligence/#195f6d121ac0

5. Dana Joseph and Daniel Newman. "Emotional Intelligence: An Integrative Meta-Analysis and Cascading Model." *Journal of Applied Psychology* 95, no. 1 (January 2010): 54–78.

6. Stéphane Côté, Katherine A. DeCelles, Julie M. McCarthy, Gerben A. Van Kleef, and Ivona Hideg. "The Jekyll and Hyde of Emotional Intelligence: Emotion-Regulation Knowledge Facilitates Both Prosocial and Interpersonally Deviant Behavior." *Psychological Science* 22, no. 8 (August 1, 2011): 1073–1080.

7. Martin Kilduff, Dan S. Chiaburu, and Jochen I. Menges. "Strategic Use of Emotional Intelligence in Organizational Settings: Exploring the Dark Side." *Research in Organizational Behavior* 30 (2010): 129–152.

8. Robert Vischer, Conrad Fiedler, Heinrich Wölfflin, Adolf Goller, Adolf Hildebrand, August Schmarsow, Harry Francis Mallgrave, and

Eleftherios Ikonomou. *On the Optical Sense of Form: A Contribution to Aesthetics, in Empathy, Form, and Space: Problems in German Aesthetics, 1873–1893 (Texts and Documents Series).* Getty Center for the History of Art, December 1, 1993, pp. 89–123.

9. Janet B. Kellett, Ronald H. Humphrey, and Randall G. Sleeth. "Empathy and Complex Task Performance: Two Routes to Leadership." *The Leadership Quarterly* 13, no. 5 (October 2002): 523–544.

INDEX